UNDER THE NEON SKY

A Las Vegas Doorman's Story

JAY RANKIN

UNDER THE NEON SKY
A Las Vegas Doorman's Story

Jay Rankin Publishing
Contact information or personal appearances,
Jay@JaysLasVegas.com or visit www.JaysLasVegas.com

Hardcover:
ISBN 10: 0-9842109-0-3
ISBN 13: 978-0-9842109-0-9

PaperBack:
ISBN 10: 0-9842109-1-1
ISBN 13: 978-0-9842109-1-6

Interior Book Design by www.KarrieRoss.com

Library of Congress Cataloging-in-Publication Data Rankin, Jay.
Under The Neon Sky: a Las Vegas doorman's story/Jay Rankin p.cm.

Printed in the United States of America

9 8 7 6 5 4 3 2 1
First Edition

DEDICATION

This book is dedicated to the millions of tourists and conventioneers who visit Las Vegas every year and to the employees who serve them. I also want to thank the following people for their support.

Thank you, Laurie Rosin, Trudie and Sandy.

Thank you, mom and dad

Thank you, Roger

Thank you, Jaden
my wonderful little boy who I love
way beyond the moon and the stars.
You have saved me.

UNDER
THE
NEON
SKY

Wait until dark, when the mood is right. The night is about possibilities. Invite a hooker to the blackjack table. Drop an extra hundred bucks on your bet. Order more drinks than you can handle. The forbidden makes Vegas unforgettable.

The Strip is dangerous. Like a jungle, exotic creatures materialize, and their beauty seduces, but they are predators, and their poison is lethal.

I watch the people and am bewitched by their downfall. I know Las Vegas is tearing me apart, but I crave the excitement. It's the only place where I feel intensely alive, even as it kills me.

The Strip stabs me with bolts of neon twenty-four hours a day, seven days a week. The power of flashing red, blue, orange, green, yellow, and white jolts me into existence. People shimmer with an inner light. The colors and sounds grow distinct, then overwhelming. The smells of the Strip tell me who I am, what to do, where to stand, when to jump out of the way.

I used to hate working nights. I felt alone and frightened. The guests are unpredictable and often crazy. Gradually, though, I became part of the Vegas night.

I can't leave this place. Why try? I've got nothing to lose. The dreams my wife, Cassy, and I brought to Las Vegas are tumbling across the cold Mojave. My soul is numb, my body's shot, my head is pounding, and I'm twitching like some nervous, fucked-up kid. When I look into the mirror, I see blond hair shot with gray and blue eyes dulled by exhaustion. My body is losing its strength. I know I should get the hell out, but tonight is about possibilities for me, too. I feel lucky. Las Vegas is giving me another chance.

I open my car window and inhale deeply—a ritual on my way to the MGM Grand. I exit at Tropicana Boulevard and nose into bumper-to-bumper traffic. I check the dashboard clock as I creep past New York, New York. Shit. I can't be late for work, not after being suspended for almost punching my supervisor..

My grip tightens on the steering wheel. My head throbs and my heart pounds. I am officially in work mode.

I fish around for the Vicodin in my duffel. I promised Cassy to cut back, but I don't have to answer to her anymore, and fuck it, tonight doesn't count. Tonight is the Sound and the Fury. Fight night.

Everyone is hopped up for the Holyfield-Tyson rematch. Fifteen thousand people will be at ringside in the MGM Grand's Garden Arena, and I'm told one-hundred fifty thousand more thrill seekers will crowd inside to gawk at celebrities.

The Grand comes into view. Everywhere I look is pandemonium and armies of patrolling police. Media trucks and city-services vehicles form barricade lines across the hotel driveway. Soon I will stand in the midst of this, at the entrance to the hotel.

I wonder if my partner, T-bone, got here, and if he has, how hopped up he is on drugs. He got rammed by a taxi two days ago and isn't doing too great.

I pop a couple painkillers and repeat my mantra. *Stay out of trouble, Jay. Just stay the fuck out of trouble.* Human Resources gave me official notification: One more complaint in my folder, and I lose my job.

Terrible foreboding fills me. Tyson attracts a dangerous crowd. Rappers claim him as their own. So do the two most notorious gangs in Los Angeles and New York, the Bloods and the Crips. Those guys are fuckin' out of control. They've been partying since their jet touched down at McCarran. If I lose my temper, they'll beat me down to my bones. If I show my fear, I'm a dead man, and no one will care. These maniacs are big spenders, and that's all that counts in this town. I've got to act cool. It ain't easy, though, wearing a stupid safari uniform, a ridiculous helmet, and tasseled knee socks.

I manage to swing my car into the employee parking lot. A thug I recognize as an off-duty cop blocks the way and scowls at me through the windshield. Then he waves me forward with a meaty hand. "Yo, Jay! Your mob wagon threw me for a second there."

I own a Lincoln Mark VII. The mob loves the Lincoln Mark series, and I take a lot of shit for owning one, even though mine looks like hell from parking in the lot. The sun seared the paint off the hood and roof, and the blowing sand stripped the finish off the body.

Valets are stealing employee spaces for guests' cars, but I finally find a place, grab my duffel, and run to the staff entrance. If T-bone came in, he will need my help out front. His shift starts earlier than mine, and he's probably been going nuts for a couple hours already.

I pass security guards on full alert. Movie stars, famous athletes, and politicians in ringside seats get off on the big stakes and bloody spectacle. They won't cause trouble, but they need protection.

Inside, I take the stairs two at a time and run through the Bell Department, a cavernous room off the front of the hotel. It holds all the luggage for guests checking in or out. Thousands of suitcases and garment bags pack the shelf space and pile high on the floor. I squeeze through the labyrinth to my small locker and change into my uniform as fast as I can.

On my way to the porte cochere I don't see the hundreds of bell carts. They're all in use. The bellmen are earning their tips tonight, just as T-bone and I will earn ours—two weeks' worth in a single night.

I arrive a couple minutes early to where I've been standing for years, at the maw of the largest hotel in the world. Tens of thousands of people have passed by me. Most look brain dead except for their pleasure-seeking synapses. The men remind me of vampires. They sweep down one side of the porte cochere, then pivot and head back, hunting for girls, games, and trouble.

One whiff of their breath exposes just about everything. Garlic reveals one set of facts; scotch relates something else entirely. Same with a cigarette or big Havana. I construct the guests piecemeal, every detail adding to the portrait, purpose, and propensities. Is he wearing snug custom clothes or loose, casual duds? Are his hands dirty from coins or chips? Are his fingernails manicured? What about shoes, hairstyle, age, cologne, gait, jewelry, tone, body language, teeth, expression?

Once I put the bits together, I know exactly who these people are. It's not a game; it's survival. In a city without boundaries, I have a chance to defend myself by knowing instantly, accurately, who's coming and going. I marvel at how much visitors believe they can get away with here. Sooner or later, though, everyone pays.

Some of the valets and doormen wear bulletproof vests on nights like this, but I won't. I could never do my spins and kicks strapped into a chest protector. My routine in the MGM Grand's driveway earns me the big bucks, and that's the only reason I'm here. I'm referred to as a "hotel ambassador." I'm a doorman— an anonymous, forty-something, theme-park actor. I can't justify what I do. I can open any door in Vegas and procure anything a visitor might want.

I fight my way through regiments of police. Thousands of people surge into the lobby and casino entrance. Never have I seen a bigger crowd, although most types are familiar: Beverly Hills mixed with gangstas, agents, cronies, wannabes, informers, and hookers. We're going to need more ambulances.

The ornate stanchion ropes that define the cab-line boundaries are gone. In their place are galvanized-steel girders twelve feet long and four feet high. If these babies don't keep the mob moving in the right direction, I don't know what will.

The porte cochere roof and the hotel facade that's ten feet behind me trap the roar of voices and cars engines and then amplify it tenfold. Rip currents of taxi fumes, cigar smoke, hot tires, and carbon monoxide take me under. A coagulation of grease, oil, and road-kill stuck to the undercarriages pins me down.

Stay focused, Jay. No margin for error. Drinking plus Gambling multiplied by Loss of Sleep equals Disaster.

T-bone glares at me. "'Bout time you got here, Rankin!" He's heaving huge, hard-sided luggage from a limousine.

I don't ask how he's feeling. His pain is obvious, and he's limping. His speech is rapid-fire and sloppy from drugs.

"This is like th' old days, with Wingy and Meyer and Ash and Roughhouse Rothman."

"Yeah, good, T-bone." I remember the big, healthy man he used to be and wonder if he thinks the sacrifice has paid off.

Now I turn to the couple at the head of the cab line. I recognize a Japanese high roller with a tall, slender Asian woman on his arm. She is young, maybe in her twenties, and she wears a stunning red, white, and blue cocktail dress with a single strap.

"Where are you folks headed tonight?" I inquire with a perfect balance of deference and enthusiasm as I summon a taxi.

I wait for an answer. They step to the side. The man grabs her long, black hair and yanks her down to her knees on the pavement. She is completely still, and for a moment they look like two dancers. I am confused. Is this performance art? A promo for some new show? I move closer, trying to make sense of the tableau.

Very slowly, grasping her hair in his fist, he pulls her face close to his crotch. What the fuck is happening? It still seems theatrical but now more like a snuff film. I squint at the woman, looking for a clue. Her mascara is smeared with her tears.

He encircles her graceful neck with one hand, and winds her hair around his other, then forces her head back, back. I am afraid he is going to snap her neck. I look around. Doesn't anyone else see what's happening? I don't want to intervene—not when I'm already on probation with HR. Jesus, no one's watching.

"Hey!" I shout, and spring toward them.

The man stops and impales me with his piercing gaze. I pull up short and watch as he slowly, deliberately, puts his arm around the woman and helps her to stand. Then they float out of my sight into the Vegas night.

I feel as if I might throw up. I need a moment to collect myself.

Behind me, people jam the lobby but will have to make room for the newcomers T-bone and I are helping from limousines and taxicabs. I fantasize that the new arrivals use a steel girder as a battering ram.

The hookers are out in force. New Jersey Rick knows all the in-house hookers. I am not that familiar, but I can pick 'em out of a crowd. Hookers are young, beautiful, and a lot smarter than you'd expect. We're all the same here on the street—humping for dollars.

T-bone is from back East, like almost everyone else working here. I'm from California—a Jew in the midst of Catholics, Evangelical Christians, and Mormons. I have a master's degree in Psychology, which doesn't mean I'm less crazy or self-destructive than anyone else, but I can see when someone's about to cross the line into ruin. I can't do anything to stop them—or myself.

Vegas is carefully constructed to propel visitors toward disaster. Most guests are in freefall. Naïve, unsuspecting, they have no defense. I witness the assisted suicide every night; I've seen it a million times. I'm almost guaranteed to be there when the thrill ends.

I turn to the next people in the cab line. Their backs are to me. "Where are you folks headed tonight?" The cab is already waiting, choking me in a fog of fumes. My eyes and lungs burn. My vision blurs, and instinctively I hold my breath. I'll do it hundreds of times before the night's over. Learning how to breathe in this city requires practice. After all these years, the atmosphere has become corporate, but the air is the same as when Meyer Lansky, Moe Dalitz, and Bugsy Siegel called the shots. Intimidation rules. Strength gets the respect.

T-bone and I have been friends for years. He likes my dangerous temper. People are afraid to push me. That's why I almost beat my supervisor half to death.

I want to keep my job. When work gets intense, like tonight, I can't think about my shitty life. I can make thousands on a fight night, so I start my act: spinning, sliding, waving my arms, and

pulling out every sly, slick trick I've learned from years on the
job. T-bone and I draw crowds with our performance under the
porte cochere. Tourists videotape us working at triple speed.

A tall, beautiful hooker passes by, and she winks at me.
I smile back. Her skirt is slit up the sides to her smooth thighs,
and her neckline plunges, all nude inside. The backless dress
shows off the dimples on her gorgeous ass. I wish she would take
me away.

"How you doin' tonight, Angel?" I ask.

"I'm so-o-o good," she says from whatever high she's on.
Her joint's gone out. A man materializes with a lighter.
She smiles at him, forgets about him, then turns back to me.
"My God, the last fight night I must have done twenty-five guys
in twenty-four hours. Know what I mean?"

"No."

She scans the lobby over my shoulder. "Of course it's nothing I'd care to do every day"—she laughs, a low chime—"but
I made a lot of money."

"I'm sure."

She takes a long, strong hit off the joint. "I worry about the
real crazies. We never know what's in a human heart."

Another hit and then blows the sweet smoke in my face. I try
to catch it. I wonder if we're on camera. I don't want to get into
trouble for talking with Angel.

She looks me up and down. "You should get some dinner.
You look a little on edge."

"Because I'm fucked."

"Like all of us." She takes one more hit and then drops the
roach in her jeweled evening bag.

I see she has a wad of bills already.

She sends looks over at T-bone. "You have plenty on your
hands."

She undulates into the lobby. If a girl is smart like Angel, she can have it all—a shelf-long collection of little black books plus a husband in the backyard and a couple of kids in Little League.

"Heads up, Jay!" T-bone shouts, and I turn just in time to avoid a tall gentleman in eveningwear throwing up at the curb beside me.

"Fuck you!" some dude behind me yells.

A fight breaks out. Just what the street needs. Two more violent drunks. I search the mob for a security cop, but none is in sight.

I watch the men swing at each other, and I brace myself. I've been hit by a stray punch or two. I turn away to open a taxi door, still expecting an uppercut to graze my temple. A moment later I turn back to see the opponents have settled their differences and are hugging each other. Jesus Christ.

The odors get denser, and the noise intensifies. I'm deafened by paradise. Coins filling up metal slot trays. Screams. Car horns. I have to yell to be heard. In a few hours my throat will be raw.

I reach for the whistle in my pocket. I lower the nylon cord around my neck and then clench the small plastic noisemaker between my teeth. My profession's one piece of inventory. Stress causes me to destroy one or more whistles every week. I lock my jaw and grind the whistle between my teeth. At this moment black plastic shards fill my mouth. I spit out the pieces and reach for one of the three new whistles in my pocket. It's that kind of night and that type of crowd. I'm filled with dread.

I look at my watch. Tyson and Holyfield are starting to go at it in the massive MGM Grand's arena. The arena holds over fifteen thousand, and the prizefight is not the only attraction: Tom Jones, EFX, and La Femme are performing in the Grand's nightclubs. The moment the shows are over, the masses will pour outside, and the bedlam will worsen.

"I ain't waiting in no fucking cab line!"

Gee, what a surprise. A loudmouthed moron who doesn't think he has to wait with the little people. The standard drill begins: Joey G. hurries from the valet station and relieves me of cab line. I step to the side to deal with the troublemaker.

This one's tall and big boned, with coarse features and spotty hygiene. He breathes hotly in my face. Chicken cacciatore and beer, men's cologne from a drugstore. That means he's an asshole.

"I'm sorry, sir," I state matter-of-factly, "but we've got a system here. If you want a cab, you will have to take your turn."

Mr. Gorilla shoves me and opens his long coat. I know what's next. I look down to see a shiny thirty-eight tucked in his pants.

"Ya see dat? Ya t'ink ya can find me a ride now?"

Doormen learned how to handle this shit during our training. Sharkey warned us from the front of the classroom, "If you lose control even for a split second, it's all over. The job is all about control."

Well, fuck that, I decide. For me it's all about money. I'll make $1500 or more on tips tonight. If I keep socking it away, I might make it out of this town.

"I'll see what I can do." I look at him with meaning.

He understands. Grinning down at me, he reaches into an inside pocket and pulls out a roll of bills. He peels off several twenties and stuffs them into my shirt pocket.

I feign surprise and signal for a taxi to find us. I make my way back to the cab line, where I hand Joey one of my twenties. "Thanks, man," I say.

"Fuh-ged aboud it." He tucks the bill in his pocket.

Kenny, one of the bellhops and not always trustworthy, hurries over. His blue eyes glitter with excitement. "All three judges give the first two rounds to Holyfield. Tyson is furious."

He scurries away before I can respond.

T-bone appears at my side. "You look like crap."

"I feel it. You do, too. How are you holding up?"

"I'm hurting, man. Can hardly move. The doc prescribed painkillers, and I told HR I need the pills if I'm gonna work."

"So you don't have to take a sick leave?" I'm amazed he is able to stand without crutches or a walker.

"I think my back could be broken, but I'm trying not to take days off."

"You're fucked up. If you're so seriously injured, you need to take care of yourself."

"Hey, we're all shot and runnin' on empty," he says. "But I'm runnin' it for all it's worth, Bro. The crowd'll be throwing hundreds at us all night. Nothing else matters." His eyes begin to glaze. "Don't you love it, man? Welcome to the real world, right?"

"It's not real, and I don't love it."

"Here. Stand still. This'll help." He faces me and grabs each of my earlobes between his thumb and forefinger. "Jay," he says, talking like Jesus, "think how you felt when you were a little boy, when you had no worries and no pain." He counts aloud, from one-one thousand to five-one thousand, while squeezing my earlobes harder and harder. Just when I can't stand the pain anymore, he lets go.

"You're one fucked-up dude," I tell him.

"I may be fucked up, but you need to relax."

Kenny interrupts, wearing a grin that shows his gums. "Tyson got Holyfield in a clinch and bit off a chunk of his ear. Holyfield's bleedin' all over—"

"Did they stop the fight?" I ask. If so, T-bone and I have to get cranking.

Words spill from Kenny's mouth. "The doc says the fight can go on. Holyfield went to his corner, and Tyson attacked him from behind. The crowd is apeshit, man!"

I turn back to the cab line. At the front a pair of young lovers are going at it. Writhing, they stumble into me, his hands busy under her skirt. She thrusts her pelvis forward.

Suddenly the masses morph into one huge, uncontrollable monster. Where the hell are the police?

Kenny appears. "Tyson just bit a bigger chunk from Holyfield's other ear, and then he took a swing at a cop who jumped into the ring. The crowd turned savage, man. Everyone was throwing stuff at Tyson. Swear to God, it's scary in there."

"Kenny, is the fight over?"

"Listen! Fights broke out in the stands, and the cops start dragging the assholes out. Then some moron wings a full bottle of water at Tyson, and Tyson goes after *him*."

"Kenny, for Chrissakes! Is the fight over?" T-bone yells. "Tell us!"

"Duh-uh. What do you think? The ref disqualified Tyson." Kenny shakes his head and walks away. T-bone goes back to his area.

I hear a weird buzzing. Cops appear by the door and talk among themselves. Don't they hear it? The first spectators from the arena hurry through, looking over their shoulders. The cops fan out.

T-bone and I exchange glances. He points to his ear and shrugs. He hears it, too. What is it? I'm sure one of the fifteen-thousand boxing fans will give me the lowdown.

A man stomps by us. He's enraged. "Muthafucker bit his fuckin' ear off!"

T-bone looks at me. I don't like seeing fear on his face. He's a former marine. Nothing scares him. He comes to stand next to me. "Whaddya think we should do?"

"Don't know, we better be ready for just about anything."

Paolo comes running over to us from his valet's station. He looks frightened. What the fuck does he have to be scared about? Some very big, bad-ass guys with puny brains are on his payroll. His lips move, but I can't understand what he is saying. Suddenly the depth of the crisis hits me.

"Keep your eyes open," I tell T-bone. "I've got your back covered."

T-bone smiles but doesn't look convinced. I don't blame him. The rumbling inside the lobby reminds me of a tornado or a tsunami.

"Don't worry," I say. "We've done this before. Sort of. We're the workhorses, man. We're the best. Remember that!" I pat him gently on the back, careful not to hurt him.

He nods and makes it back to his place.

Paolo stops beside me and shakes his head as he sees what's become of T-bone. "The crowd is going crazy in there, tearing the place apart," he says. "I'm getting the fuck outta here, man, and I suggest you do the same and take T-bone with you."

"Yeah, well, that might be an option for someone who's not on notice," I mutter, watching as he jogs in the direction of employee parking.

The sound inside the hotel escalates to a jet spiraling to earth. Screams mixed with glass exploding erupt from the lobby. I see a fast-moving crowd, thousands of people, rushing toward the doors, coming straight at me. I stand paralyzed. My brain won't work. Then my survival instinct sends me hurtling to the side, away from the force of this human tidal wave.

"They're shooting!" a woman shrieks.

"They got guns!"

"God help us!"

Everyone is screaming so loudly, I can't hear the gunshots.

The lobby doors burst open. T-bone and I look at each other in horror. They're all running for their life. Thousands of people race past me, the fastest ones push to the fore and knock down anyone in their way. Hundreds of people disappear underfoot.

I can't breathe. Nothing stops the momentum—not even the steel girders. Ripped from their frames, the reinforced barricades shoot up like missiles, then crash down. I hear the sickening snap of bones.

Cops draw their firearms and aim high, trying to slow the mob. I watch in disbelief as the police, too, disappear under the force of the charge.

My eyes fix on a body facedown on the pavement just three feet from the tip of my shoes. Hundreds trample him before they disappear into the darkness. Taxis push through the crowd. A woman lies crumpled at my feet, run over by a panicky driver.

I don't see T-bone anywhere. I call out for him. I walk blindly under the porte cochere, barely able to keep focused. Thirty or forty people are sprawled on the pavement in spreading pools of blood. No one moves. I want to help them, but I need to find my partner.

The shrill of the hotel fire alarms cut through the night air. Fire trucks, ambulances, and squads converge on the hotel. A SWAT van roars into the driveway, and people part for it as they are able. A half-dozen well-armed officers jump out and dash into the lobby.

"*T-bone!*" I scream. "*T-bone!*"

I won't leave until I find him. And when I do, I promise myself, I'll get him home, or I'll get him help, or I'll get him buried.

CHAPTER TWO

"Hey, Cassy," I called up the stairs, "will you give me a hand here?"

I wanted to unpack the new kitchen cabinets, but I needed another set of hands to anchor the box while I pulled out the merchandise.

"Let me do that, man." Sam appeared from out of nowhere, and suddenly I was steadying the box while he wrestled out the packing foam and the solid ash cabinet frames. Sam was like that—ready to volunteer with so much enthusiasm, you'd think his name was on the deed.

Part of my appreciation for Sam was that he lived a respectable life. In Las Vegas, most people fucked up with a vengeance. He made a point of helping as much as he could— partly because his wife was expecting their first baby and he could use the money, and partly because we worked well together and enjoyed each other's company. He and Sheila lived nearby, which made it easy for him and me to train together at the gym and just goof around.

Cassy's voice floated down the stairwell. "I'll be there in a sec."

She came down the stairs, walking carefully on stiletto heels. She'd brought her skimpy costume to our spec house, so she could change into it and go directly to her job. "What do you want, honey?"

"When you're wearing that outfit," I told her, "you don't even have to ask." Her long black hair and beautiful green eyes underscored how hot she looked in her cocktail waitress's outfit, even as she unceremoniously yanked at the short-shorts that kept riding up her ass.

"I'm glad *you* like it. I hate this thing!" She looked up, her eyes shooting sparks. "And if either of you so much as laughs, you'll get my fist down your throat."

Sam held up his hands defensively. "Whoa, there. I'm not going to laugh. Are *you* thinking of laughing, Jay?"

"And gag on my molars? Shit, no, man. Cassy always means what she says."

The phone rang, and my wife, holding her breasts so they wouldn't bounce out of her bodice, hurried down the rest of the stairs. She grabbed the handset before the answering machine kicked in. "Yes, he's right here, Mrs. Levine. Just one moment."

She handed me the receiver, then nervously pressed her hands to her cheeks and waited.

"This is Jay Rankin."

"And this is Shirley Levine, Jay, from the MGM Grand Human Resources office. I'm pleased to say we've selected you as one of our guest ambassadors. Are you still interested in the position?"

"Yes! Yes, very much!"

"Excellent. Please report to training tomorrow morning, on site, at eight-thirty. Signs will direct you where to park and where to report. Plan to spend the whole day."

I hung up, dazed, and looked from my wife to my friend. Even though the Grand was hiring thousands of people, the competition was unbelievably stiff, especially for the better-paying jobs. Senior management was already in place, filled by the corporate office with individuals who had a solid history with Kirk Kerkorian's organization. As for the rest of the openings, the best would go to applicants backed by the most influential connections or underwritten with the heftiest bribes.

My contacts in the casino industry and among politicians were of little consequence. So how'd I make the cut? I had hosted a popular local television program that focused on the Las Vegas business community. Against all the odds, the program conferred enough hometown-celebrity status to win a job. Even more incredible, during the group interviews, televisions in the huge room happened to be broadcasting a rerun of my show, focusing on the construction of the new MGM Grand hotel. When the interviewer told me I looked familiar, I pointed toward the nearest bank of monitors.

"You got the job?" Cassy asked.

"I got it," I said, almost afraid to smile.

Cassy and I hugged each other, and then Sam's long arms pulled me to his six-foot, six-inch frame. "I'm happy for you, man," he said, and thumped me on the back.

"I'll put in a good word for you as soon as I can," I promised.

"I know you will."

"Does this mean you're a doorman?" Cassy asked.

"I'm not sure. She called me a 'guest ambassador.'"

"He don't know!" Sam guffawed.

"What do you think that means?" Cassy asked.

"I think I got the job as a doorman!" I shouted over Sam's whooping.

"You best find out before you sign on the line, brother," he said.

A horn blared in the driveway—or what would be the driveway when our spec house was finished—and I went to the window. A stunning redhead sat behind the wheel of a lavender BMW convertible.

"You riding with someone?" I asked Cassy.

"She's *my* ride," Sam said, fully aware of the double meaning, and went off to gather his tools.

I raised my eyebrows at Cassy, but her shrug told me his lady friend was none of our business. She and I had always disagreed on this core philosophy. I'd always believed I was my brother's keeper—that we all were, to some extent. My years as a probation officer concretized that notion. Every day in the probation camp, I worked with one poor slob after another who had turned his life into dog shit. I always wondered what if they had a friend who'd said, "Listen, asshole, here's the line. Don't fucking cross it!"

Sam was not some kid in need of guidance, though. He was a good-looking black man in his early thirties. He and his beautiful wife were serious athletes, and to me that meant he understood discipline. Sam had been the United States Cruiserweight Kickboxing Champion, for Christ sake. Was any sport more demanding? When he didn't measure up in the ring, he couldn't fall back on teammates to protect his ass.

Naw, Sam had nothing going on with the redhead. I was sure of it. If he did, he'd have told me.

"These are beautiful," Cassy said, bending over to run her hand down the cabinet face.

"These, too," I said, grabbing her ass and squeezing.

She yelped and wheeled around and put her arms around my neck.

"These, too." I cupped her breasts and nuzzled her cleavage.

She smiled, squirming. "This is good, Jay."

"The cabinets?" I murmured, licking her. Her nipples were hard. "We made a good decision picking out the knobs?"

"*Mmmm*. So good." She rubbed against me. "And now you know what I'm going to do to you?"

"What, honey?"

"Piss you off and go to work." She peeled herself off me. Her face was flushed.

"Yeah, well, just don't finish this off later with someone else, all right?"

"You don't have to worry," she said. "We're back on track now."

After Cassy left, I stood in the sunlit silence and admired the bones of the house surrounding me. A work in progress, full of hopes and dreams. We had done the same thing in Connecticut—built a house with the intention of selling it at a profit. We'd failed miserably.

Maybe this one will be one rung up the ladder to a better life. Las Vegas was booming, so I decided to build a million-dollar spec house. The profit would allow Cassy and me to have our own nice home someday. More than constructing a house, I hoped we'd rebuild our life and marriage. Already we were creating a new identity in the community and making friends.

Getting the job with the Grand against such unbelievable odds was an omen. The next few years would be good for us. Nothing could go wrong.

"You people have been selected from many thousands of applicants to be the ambassadors of the MGM Grand. You'll be on the front line of the largest hotel in the world, with over five thousand guest rooms. You will at all times carry yourself with dignity and professionalism. You must be in total control of your area."

I sat in a classroom with the nine other doormen-to-be, listening to our instructor. We were all different from one another except for gender. Not a woman among us. Sharkey, as I nicknamed our supervisor because he had small, dark eyes and too many teeth, had himself been a doorman for many years, and he was very clear about his expectations.

I glanced around at the other trainees. We had already survived a background check for military records, driving records, police records, and credit reports. That morning we had endured an exhausting four-hour trek through hundreds of underground tunnels, cubicles, and booths, where we sat for photos and received ID cards, nametags, badges, medical cards, and an employee number. We tucked away a car sticker for parking, and we juggled brochures, tapes, and manuals.

We gave up a lock of our hair for drug testing. Some users had shaved their head to avoid the test but were forced to provide a hair sample from their groin. Rumor had it that one-third of all hotel applicants failed this test.

During the processing, I got acquainted with some of the other ambassadors. One was a mountain of a man with a friendly, large personality. With three hundred pounds packed on a six-foot, four-inch frame, he inadvertently inflicted pain whenever he shook hands with us. We all decided to nickname him D-Man. The *D* was for dinosaur.

Another was a part-time university professor who needed extra income. Highly intelligent and levelheaded, he had a calming effect on me whenever we had an opportunity to talk.

At the other end of the spectrum was the unbelievably hyper T-Bone, whose avocation was holistic medicine. When I looked into his eyes, I thought he should cut back on his vitamins.

A weightlifter and ex-marine, he had worked as a doorman at a five-star hotel in California.

A guy from Chicago was the clown. Another, whom I nick-named Weasel, had an arrogant attitude and a wise-guy smile.

"People," Sharkey continued now, pacing the front of the classroom, "this is the new Las Vegas. In the old days casino owners were, uh, open-minded about running a hotel. When a customer accompanied his request with money, the staff filled every demand, including the purchase of illegal drugs or the procurement of a lovely hooker."

He paused, then said harshly, "Those days are over! If you are caught doing any of these sidelines, you will be dismissed instantly!

"While we're on the subject of how to get dismissed. Be late to work, I'll fire you. Fail to clock in, I'll fire you. If I ever find out you have yelled at a guest . . ."

He looked at us expectantly.

"You'll fire us," we drawled obediently.

"That's correct!" He looked happy.

The room was silent as we all stared at Sharkey.

"How will I evaluate your job performance?" he asked. "Video cameras are everywhere. Security as well as management will be watching you. And believe me, the guests themselves can always be counted on to let us know when you are out of line."

He dug in his trouser pocket. "Now I am going to teach you how to take a dollar."

He's got to be kidding, I thought.

"You will open the taxi or limo door with this hand." He raised his left hand. "Then if you see the guest trying to hand you a tip, you will take it with your right hand and thank the person. Is this clear?"

One of the doormen raised his hand.

Sharkey looked at him. "What?"

"Well, I just wanted to know if it's okay to do it the other way around because I'm left-handed."

Sharkey took out a pad of paper and made a note to himself. This made Lefty very nervous.

"Do whatever is comfortable for you. Do you think you can do that?" Sharkey asked sarcastically. "Because if you can't, then maybe we can get you transferred to another department."

The man bobbed his head. "Yes, sir!"

"Because of lawsuits, never touch people," Sharkey went on, "other than to shake hands." He leaned toward his new target and sneered. "Right or left hand."

The fellow looked down at the desk.

"Looking like Dustin Hoffman in *Midnight Cowboy* will get you dismissed," Sharkey continued. "You are to bathe every single day. You are to shave every day. Your hair, skin, teeth, fingernails, uniform, and shoes must look clean and neat. No earrings, no visible tattoos.

"Answering questions about our hotel and our city will be a big part of your job. The more you know, the better the response will be from our guests. Study guidebooks and learn what our city has to offer. Learn everything you can about this hotel.

"If the guest wants a restaurant recommendation for a good steak or piece of fresh fish, do not send him anywhere outside this hotel. With a total of eight fine-dining restaurants, five casual restaurants, and three cafés, we have everything a guest might need all right here. Our celebrity chefs include Wolfgang Puck, Mark Miller, and Emeril Lagasse. *Bang!*" he shouted, impersonating Emeril, and we all jumped.

Sharkey grinned, then took a deep breath. I thought I saw slits on his neck open and close.

As the days passed and the training continued, I learned exactly how complex the MGM Grand would be. The mega-resort was a group of several businesses operating under one roof: the restaurant business, the hotel business, the casino business, the entertainment business, the retail shops, and all the other services that make up a full-blown Vegas property. We were taught rules, regulations, procedures, and policies.

The more Sharkey talked, the more confused I became. We furiously wrote down statistics as he dictated: "No place in Las Vegas offers as many entertainment venues as the Grand. The Hollywood Theatre presents major performing acts. The Grand Garden Arena hosts sports events and musical superstars. Studio 54 recreates the classic New York disco and offers music and dancing until the early morning hours.

"Make sure the guests visit the resort's astonishing Lion Habitat. Onsite amenities include the incredible convention building, full-service day spa, wedding chapel, business center, large swimming-pool area. Even the parking structure, when built, will be the world's largest.

"The casino is almost one-hundred, seventy-two thousand square feet. It has thirty-seven hundred slot machines.

"We're going to tour the casino, and I want everyone to stay together. If you wander off, I won't come looking for you. Getting lost is no excuse for showing up late for having your uniform fitted. I've scheduled that to take place right after the tour.

"When the seamstress tells you she is done, I want you to go home and think about what we've discussed this week." His gaze was lethal. "Make sure it sinks in."

During the tour I decided to wander from my group and check things out on my own. I got lost. The place was huge. I searched for something I could use a landmark, but in the vastness, everything looked unfamiliar. I asked every staff member I met for help, but their directions sent me farther into the monster's belly.

I was thirsty, and my feet hurt. I was about to use my cell phone to call for help. I should have listened to Sharkey.

My savior proved to be a little woman on the household staff. She was vacuuming the new carpet in a corridor. She spoke almost no English, but she took hold of my hand and walked me to the exit.

CHAPTER THREE

"Maybe you should print up a map of the hotel," Sam said. "Just so you could find the bathroom from your work station."

"That's actually a great idea."

He and I had just bought granite for the spec-home counter-tops, and now he was driving me back to the Grand.

"As soon as I begin to feel familiar with a room or an area, the place gets a makeover with paint or signs, and I can't recognize it anymore. I'm always asking for directions, but no one seems to be able to help me."

"Everyone's lost?" he asked, chuckling.

"Some worse than others. They're staggering around, hopeless. Their eyes keep rolling back in their head." I smiled at the memory. "They never should've been hired in the first place."

I supposed it was cool for the Grand to be gargantuan, but I couldn't help but wish it were smaller. Did any resort need to have eighty elevators or a casino that could hide Delaware? I felt diminished by its dehumanizing bulk, but the man behind the project would feel just the opposite. Kirk Kerkorian was the king of the colossal resort. The Grand would be his third hotel in Vegas, and in their day, the old MGM and the International had also been the world's largest.

Kerkorian was a self-made billionaire. No one believed he could make Vegas a destination for families and convention-goers, but he hadn't risen from being a pro boxer to one of the wealthiest men in the world by dreaming small. I respected him for that, and I liked that he drove himself around town in a mod-est, powder-blue Buick Skylark station wagon. I fantasized about meeting him, but my job as a doorman would not guarantee that happening. For a few minutes, though, the idea of it occupied my mind.

I turned to Sam. "I can't believe how nervous I am about this job!"

"Why, man? You've got to be smarter than the other door-men. You've got a fucking graduate degree in psychology."

"I'm the only doorman who hasn't had hotel experience."

"You're just having the jitters before starting a new job. Perfectly normal. I'm sure the other guys feel the same way."

"Yeah, you're probably right," I told him. But I wondered if they were also feeling lost and alone.

"You'll settle down as soon as opening day is behind you, man."

"I'd better! I wouldn't want to feel like this on a long-term basis. No fucking way."

When Sam dropped me off, I reported to Wardrobe. As I walked downstairs, I reminded myself to focus on the positive. I had learned in grad school that the physical manifes-tations of anxiety and excitement were identical. I reminded myself I was *excited,* thrilled, in fact, about working at the Grand.

I made myself admire all the different and colorful uniforms designed for the dealers, housekeeping staff, front-desk personnel, and valets. Especially entrancing were the cocktail servers' one-piece costumes with a pushup bra. In lush, deep jewel tones, the outfits exposed as much as possible of the women's long legs, sleek and shapely in hosiery.

"They really look fine," D-man said, standing at my shoulder in the vast Wardrobe area. "In fact, these women look so fine, not even a safari hat could ruin their sex appeal."

I laughed. "Yeah, our costumes suck."

"I like that they don't have to wear a wig," he added, eyes still on the servers. "I'd rather see a woman's real hair, all soft and shiny."

"Easy, boy," I told him.

D-man took one last, long look, and then he and I went to find the other guys.

"I'm glad I'm not the only one who hates our uniform."

"Don't you wonder about the moron who designed them?" he asked.

"Yeah. How the hell did he get hired in the first place?"

Our summer getup consisted of a safari shirt, Bermuda shorts, knee socks with a tassel, and the inevitable safari hat. Who in his right mind would wear tasseled socks with a safari hat?

The winter uniform resembled a circus ringmaster's attire. The top-hat material was stiff, and it fit tight to my skull. If the guests didn't bring on a migraine, the hat surely would. Whenever I tried on the long jacket with tails and a bowtie, I had to resist the urge to look for a whip and a couple of elephants.

D-man and I found the doormen lining up, stripped down to boxer shorts. A group of managers stood observing, Sharkey among them. He was holding up his left wrist and rotating it.

An unbelievably thick rug of dark hair pushed out from under his French cuff.

"Your watch will become your friend," he was saying, "so make sure it works, men."

"I don't see any watch," Chicago the Clown murmured. "Do you?"

We struggled to stifle our laughter.

Several seamstresses trotted in to fuss over us, as if we were bullfighters being fitted for the adoring crowds. I stood staring at myself in the mirror. A couple of childhood tics and twitches briefly plagued me. I needed a drink.

"Please don't make me wear this in public," I moaned to the seamstress.

"You are ambassador of chotel," she scolded. "These clothes give guests exchitement and cho you work here."

The seamstresses nearly drove us crazy, pulling and tucking, folding and pinning. None of our uniforms fit. Off our clothes went for more alterations, then back on and then off again. It took forever, but the other guys and I got better acquainted while we hung around.

"Hey! You know, you guys, it's critical we all drink a lot of fluids to cleanse our bodies."

We all turned to stare blankly at the hyperactive health-nut weightlifter. His name was Todd, but we'd nicknamed him T-bone because his body was like a lean piece of meat. Even in a crowd of a thousand people, everyone would notice him. His frame was big boned and muscular, and he had a Joe Palooka squared jaw, thick dark eyebrows, and piercing brown eyes. His personality was like a bright banner. And he never shut the fuck up.

"See, what we do for eight hours is stand in one place, sucking in fumes from all the cars and buses," he continued his rapid-fire dissertation. "All those toxins are bombarding our bodies! Unless we take decisive action, they will poison us and break down our immune system! We should all be on some really good vitamins and antioxidants to keep our bodies running strong! I mean, do you guys have any idea how damaging it is out there?"

He was talking faster and faster. "It's so important that we maintain our stamina and energy so we can give all our guests world-class service!"

He didn't miss a beat when a seamstress returned with his uniform. His voice got louder and his breathing quickened as he pulled on his trousers. Veins in his forehead and neck bulged, and his eyes glittered. "I can't emphasize enough how important this all is! I mean, we should be eating at least five times a day and have bottled water with us at all times! Whenever you want we can sit down, and I'll suggest some great herbs we should all be taking at least three or four times a day!"

D-man decided to step in. "Hey, T-bone, calm down a little, brother." He slung his arm around Todd and patted his chest. "You're going to give yourself a heart attack."

"I agree with T-bone," Weasel said, his eyes mere slits. "I found an herb that I take all the time because it relaxes me and gives me a buzz."

We all laughed, except for T-bone.

Sharkey slowly glided forward and circled us. "Remember, you men will be representing this hotel both in the way you look and the way you behave."

I had never stood so close to him, and I couldn't look away from his chaotically crooked teeth. Sharkey seemed to have enough choppers for two people. Jumbled rows of eyeteeth looked like so many bowling pins after a strike.

"Carry yourselves with dignity and professionalism," he continued, "or I will fire you immediately. Be a helpful and courteous ambassador, or I will fire you."

Management by intimidation, I thought. I really don't like this guy, and I am tired of the word *ambassador*.

"While we're waiting for the alterations," he went on, "I'll assign your shifts and your days off. With everyone being a new employee, no one has seniority, so we'll do it by lottery." He handed out pieces of paper and yellow half-pencils without erasers. "Write down your preferences and prioritize them as one, two, and three. I will collect the papers, then pull them at random from a hat. The order will assign you your employee seniority."

Finally! The all-important moment had arrived. I already knew what to request. Cassy and I had been devising my strategy for days. She worked the graveyard shift at Caesar's Palace—eight at night till four in the morning. If both of us could work nights, it would be great for our marriage. Maybe she'd hate her job less if it coordinated with mine and allow us free time together.

Sharkey borrowed D-man's top hat and walked around with it. We folded our slips of paper and dropped them in the hat, then Sharkey turned to face us. With enormous gravity he began. Neither of the first two doormen picked had requested a night shift. So far, so good.

T-bone's name came up third, and he got my first choice: 5 P.M. to 1 A.M. Shit.

"Fourth is . . . Jay Rankin," Sharkey said. "Your shift is seven P.M. to three A.M., Rankin."

I exchanged glances with T-bone. He and I had a significant overlap from when I arrived at seven and he left at one. Holy shit. We were partners. The guy was all over the place like buckshot, and we were fucking partners.

He grinned maniacally and gave me a thumbs-up. I tried to smile back at him while a vision popped in my head of his pouring vitamins down my throat while I landed punches on his solar plexus.

Well, at least Cassy and I would have similar schedules. That was good. And the seven-to-three shift had the potential for a great income, with crowds leaving from dinner, shows, and concerts. Yeah, I decided, it would work out okay. Besides, I got along with almost everyone, and I'd get along with T-bone.

A seamstress handed me my adjusted uniform. I shrugged it on and stared in the mirror.

"You ready!" she pronounced cheerily. "Very nice. You chansome man! Ambassador!"

Before going home, I took a detour toward the main lobby. This would be my last chance to wander around before the public invaded the Grand. The hotel's theme was the Wizard of Oz, underscoring Kerkorian's commitment to family vacations. When the youngsters would burst through the front doors, they'd stand directly opposite life-sized figures of Dorothy, the Tin Man, the Lion, and the Scarecrow. The roped-off area looked as if a piece of Kansas real estate had been plowed from the earth and transported to Vegas.

Building on the theme, the hotel had created a Yellow Brick Road leading from the lobby display. Guests who followed that path would find the elevators and restaurants. I vividly remembered the movie with Judy Garland, and now I laughed out loud, realizing that the actor who played the Wizard had also portrayed an Emerald City doorman. Ambassador.

The movie in many ways resembled my life. It had started in sepia, but as soon as Dorothy arrived in Oz, Technicolor burst onto the screen—the first, full-length, full-color feature film shown to a wide audience. After enduring the Depression, the film's impact on the public in 1939 was stunning—sort of the same way I had felt coming to Las Vegas for the first time and seeing my biological father after seven long years.

He left Mom and me when I was four years old. We moved in with her mother and sister. They said my father was a bad man who hurt my mother. I could not believe them. In my vague memories, he had always been nice to me. Through the years, I missed my father. No one explained why he had vanished or why my mom was so sick with migraine headaches or why we were so poor.

My mother took an office job. She had no money to outfit herself. She wore whatever clothes she had until everything was threadbare. I remember the backside of her skirts was shiny from wear. Our life was grim, funereal, monochromatic. I stayed in my room. I watched television. I was miserable.

Then, for no apparent reason, my father called and asked my mother if I could visit him for a weekend in Las Vegas. He would pay for my roundtrip train ticket. She said yes, and I was terrified—excited. I could not imagine what awaited me. I had never even seen pictures of Las Vegas.

During the journey from L.A., I looked out the train window and saw nothing but desert, then more of the same. As the train rolled closer to its destination, I noticed lights in the distance, in the midst of the vast darkness. How was it possible, I wondered as we pulled into the station, to invent lights in the middle of nowhere?

Then I saw him. He seemed very familiar. I remember thinking, Yes, he looks how I had pictured him. In my mind, though, the image was flat and told me nothing about the man. Being in his company answered many of my questions.

He was a gambler. His girlfriend, Coco, was a gorgeous showgirl. I fell completely in love with her. They took me to all the casinos. Everywhere we went, colors exploded around me and electricity flowed through me. Everyone was laughing! They were having fun!

Hey, wait a minute! That was not what life was about. Or was it?

Suddenly, as an eleven-year-old, I witnessed an astonishing, utterly amazing reality. My world expanded to gather in the lights, the colors, the sounds. I had to reinvent everything I knew about life, about this man who called himself my father, and about myself. Suddenly my gray world filled with new possibilities.

That weekend, my infatuation with the city took hold. It brought me back to life. It brought me back to Vegas.

CHAPTER FOUR

Now that I knew my work schedule, I needed to focus on Cassy and me. I was determined our marriage would endure.

Las Vegas wouldn't make that easy. Husbands and wives worked so many different shifts, they rarely had free time to spend with each other. As employees of the hotel industry, we wouldn't even celebrate holidays together like normal human beings. Holidays were the busiest time in a city that already operated nonstop. No employee ever had Fourth of July or New Year's Eve off. That was a given in this party town.

So was this: Let's say you are at work and your wife is alone, searching for something to do. She has to be careful and aware. In Las Vegas, the line dividing fidelity from betrayal is laser thin, and it stretches clear to the horizon. Human predators are always sniffing around, poised to pull her across. A few hours later, your wife, who means the world to you, means nothing to the hunter. She's just a faceless stranger used for a night of partying and then discarded.

And what about the wife in this hypothetical situation? Assuming she is decent and usually level-headed, she can't forget what she has done. That one stupid mistake poisons her self-concept, redefines her, and destroys her marriage. If the waywardness gave her pleasure, then she'll crave it, and that will prove her downfall. If she feels regretful, then her shame and guilt will eat away at her.

I knew this. I had witnessed it. I feared it, and it haunted me. My days off were Thursday and Friday. Cassy's weren't. She didn't have enough seniority at Caesar's to qualify for a schedule change. She wasn't happy about that —or about much of anything else, either. She went through these dark moods occasionally. I knew in time they would pass.

I tried not to contribute to Cassy's misery because of my job jitters. The other guys warned me I'd have to answer a slew of rapid-fire questions about the city, so I had begun some serious memorization of Vegas facts. Just before the mega-opening of the MGM Grand, I stretched out on our king-sized bed with a guidebook while Cassy, looking into the mirror over our dresser, dutifully attached her Caesar's Palace ponytail hairpiece. Holding her hands high caused her gold lamé bathing suit to ride up her butt. I admired her for a moment, then went back to my book, to regale her with city history.

"Hey, honey, what do you think Liberace's name is?"

"*Eee?*"

I looked up from the page. Cassy had hairpins sticking out of her mouth. "Good guess, babe. His friends call him Lee. But his first name is Walter."

"*Mmmm.*"

"He got the idea for his candelabrum from a movie about Chopin, and he bought a piano that had belonged to Chopin. And another that was George Gershwin's."

"*Hmmm.*" She used her last hairpin and began her mascara ritual. "Those must have cost him a couple of pennies. Along with all the other crap he bought." She made a rude noise and wiggled her hips. "Happy fuckin' happies."

I laughed. "Hey, let's have a little compassion for the man who makes too much money!"

Everyone in town knew Liberace's reputation as a compulsive collector. He filled warehouses with his acquisitions. Junk or antiques or treasures, Liberace called it all his "happy happies."

I read on. "It says here that when he opened at the Hilton in 1972, he was making three-hundred grand per week!"

"Are you kidding me? *I* wouldn't pay a nickel to see him. I can't stand the guy."

"Well, he appeals to little old ladies. But," I said, reading, "'no other Las Vegas headliner has made more than Liberace.'"

"More than Elvis, even?" she asked. "I don't believe it!"

"Hold on, let me look it up." I found *Presley, Elvis* in the index and went to his pages to compare salaries. "Yep. Ol' Mr. Showmanship made more dough than The King. When Elvis performed at the International, Kerkorian paid him *only* a hundred grand a week, then upped it by another twenty-five grand."

"You don't need to read me the whole book, Jay."

I heard the sudden change in her voice, but another item had caught my eye. "Just one more thing. Okay?"

"Okay," she said with exaggerated tolerance.

"Where did you suppose Elvis came up with the idea for his famous jumpsuit with pearls, beads, rhinestones—"

"Jimi Hendrix?" She struggled with her false eyelashes with one hand and the crotch of her bathing suit with the other.

"Very funny. Guess again."

"Elizabeth Taylor?"

"No . . ."

"Rock Hudson."

"Nope. Liberace!" I laughed. "Imagine! Elvis wanted to dress like fuckin' Liberace!"

"Goddamn it, Jay!" she exploded. "I'm glad you find life so goddamned amusing. I'm miserable! I've had it with this fucking costume and these fucking eyelashes and—"

"Honey, I have an idea. How about quitting tonight?"

"Quitting what?" she asked angrily, finding my face in the mirror. She had those beautiful catlike green eyes. They were what first attracted me to her.

"Quitting your job. Caesar's. You hate it, don't you?"

She rolled her eyes as if to say, Duh.

"So quit. Call and tell 'em you'll return your gold piece-of-shit uniform tomorrow and would like to pick up your paycheck while you're there."

Again she tugged at the bathing suit, but I could tell she was thinking. "Pretty short notice . . ."

"And the women you work with have earned your loyalty."

"Hah! Now *that's* funny!"

"So?"

She stood for a moment, her brows knit. "Can we afford it, with you just about to start work?"

I shrugged. "So the other doormen tell me."

A dazzling smile lit her face. "Then why the hell not?" she whooped. She yanked off her hairpiece, twirled it overhead, then launched it across the room. She dived onto the bed to give me quick kisses, then rolled over to pick up the phone from her night table.

As I listened to her conversation with her supervisor, I hoped the guys had been right about the tips. I'd always worked hard but had little to show for my efforts. I had made great friends and done a lot of laughing, but the older I got, the more I craved stability. I decided marriage would be my salvation. I promised myself that the next woman who came into my life, I'd marry her and make the relationship work. That woman had been Cassy. But Jesus, she was high maintenance.

She hung up the phone and danced her way into the bathroom. Her emotional baggage, packed tight, could fill an eighteen-wheeler built for long-distance hauling. She was quick to go on the defensive, and her harsh edge and wounding sarcasm distanced me. If she drank too much, she got sloppy and nasty. Fortunately she had the alcohol under control. Now. But these moods. . . .

Then again, security and stability were as core to Cassy as they were to me. Her upbringing and mine had been miserable. Unlike Cassy, at least I'd had a home. And my situation eventually improved, while Cassy's never did.

After a few years without my sperm-donor father for a husband, my mother met a man who proposed marriage. Her beau was willing to care for her and accept me in the deal.

At first, he and I never said much to each other, but many years later, I realized that my stepfather's contentment with the mundane provided the foundation for our security. In time, he had become my father.

I wanted to provide financial security and emotional and physical intimacy for Cassy, and now, as I heard her singing through the bathroom door, knowing how happy I had made her gave me enormous satisfaction. I would encourage her to find a job she liked. With her looks, she would land a job soon in another casino.

The bathroom door opened, filling the bedroom with fragrant steam. A fresh-faced Cassy, wearing a towel and a triumphant smile, threw herself down on the bed and covered my face with kisses.

"Oh, Gawd, Jay, those other girls I had to work with were such total bitches. Do you know how great I feel, never having to go back there?" She slid her fingers down the waistband of my sweatpants.

"I'm beginning to figure it out," I said, and reached to put the Vegas guidebook on my nightstand.

"I'm ecstatic! I have everything planned out. I want to take a couple weeks off and then I'll find a nine-to-five job."

I kissed the top of her head. "That's great, honey," I said, but I felt uneasy. If Cassy worked days and I worked nights, when would we see each other? How would we stay connected?

Finally opening day arrived. Sharkey told us to report early for last-minute briefings and a uniform check. We still did not know the final, critical layout of our work area outside the lobby doors. The crosswalk, temporary parking for the unloading of bags, taxi line, etc., all had to function smoothly for the thousands of guests passing through the porte cochere.

All week I had watched management grapple with where to locate the stanchion ropes—the thick, black ropes stretching between shining brass poles, to guide the visitors into a nice, neat line. There they would wait in an orderly fashion until they reached the head of the line and it was their turn to climb into a taxi and hand me my tip.

The day before, the challenge of the layout had taken on the full weight and gravity of the Manhattan Project, with no fewer than ten managers, supervisors, captains, and doormen embroiled in a heated debate. The layout that worked well on Monday didn't work Tuesday; what looked good Wednesday morning no longer suited on Wednesday afternoon; a so-called latest procedure Thursday was supplanted by a much newer concept Friday. I watched the poles and ropes moved, curved, lengthened, shortened, removed, replaced, bent, straightened, and twisted. Nothing stayed the same. . . except our uniforms.

Suggestions escalated to arguments and then threats. Never had I experienced such noise, enmity, and chaos. Feelings and egos were bruised. Why was everyone taking it so personally? Why was everyone so confounded by the cab line's orientation?

I prayed the managers hadn't ultimately decided to banish the stanchion ropes, cabs, and doormen. I hoped they had come to a consensus, and I would find out what it was before the resort opened for business.

Now, I walked through the employee entrance and plunged into apocalyptic confusion, with people dashing around, frantic. Construction workers furiously installed lights, hung doors, and touched up dings in the painted walls. Hammers banged, drills screamed, and people yelled for assistance and glue. Meanwhile musicians set up their band instruments and checked the maximum output of their sound equipment. Managers with sweaty faces commanded the underlings to complete every forgotten detail and solve every problem. Housekeeping staffers raced by, barely in control of stainless-steel carts laden with stacks of towels. The carts took the corners on two wheels.

I bumped into the Weasel and the Professor, who were also on the way to rendezvous with Sharkey. Just as Sam had predicted, they looked jittery. We quick-stepped into the baggage room, and Sharkey told us to line up. I found a place next to T-bone, who was bouncing lightly on the balls of his feet.

"You are under incredible scrutiny," Sharkey began. "News crews from around the world are covering this momentous event. When their cameras take aim at the A-list celebrities and athletes here for the festivities, your image may be seen in the background. Your appearance must be flawless."

"Uh, sir?" D-man raised his hand and was recognized. "Where did management position the stanchion ropes?"

We murmured in agreement, glad he'd asked.

Sharkey cleared his throat but said nothing.

Oh, Jesus, I thought.

"Management still has that under advisement—" he finally answered.

We groaned as one.

"—so why don't we go down to the porte cochere now to see what's been decided."

Exhaustion and management's lack of new opinions had settled the cab-line issue before my job was abolished. Soon the doors swung wide to welcome the public, and the taxi line quickly filled. I watched T-bone work the crowd. He put his endless energy to good use. I felt exhilarated. Maybe he'd be a good partner and not make me nuts, after all.

"We'd like to go to the Rio, please."

I turned to see five women in their late sixties, all decked out in jewels, glitter glued on their face. Expensive evening dresses flowed over Rubenesque figures. They stumbled around, laughing and being seductive with me.

"Ladies, you all look really hot tonight," I told them, and beckoned to a cab.

One of them sidled up to me. Her hair was as thick and as gold as her jewelry. She slid her arm around my waist. "What are you doing later tonight?" she asked, looking me right in the eyes.

I didn't want to offend her. I answered lightly, "You stay out of trouble, okay?"

"But I want to get into trouble," she cooed, never unlocking her gaze.

The taxi pulled up, and I helped each woman inside. Two of them handed me a dollar each. The seductress stopped and turned to me before settling into the cab. "You sure you don't want to meet me later?" She pressed a gratuity in my palm.

"I'm honored, but I'm sure," I told her, and closed the door.

As the cab drove off, I saw she had stuck a condom in my hand.

Questions came nonstop from one guest after another. I surprised myself with how much I had memorized. T-bone filled in anything I didn't know.

"How much is a taxi to the Mirage?"

"About seven or eight dollars."

"Unless the driver takes you the long way," T-bone chimed in. "Then the fare could be two or three hundred dollars."

"Is that where the volcano is?"

"Yes, ma'am," I said.

"What time does it go off?"

"Every hour."

"How long does it last?"

"A little over five minutes." So far, so good.

"Is it safe?"

"Yes, now that they've learned to control the flow of the lava. It doesn't go down the street anymore."

T-bone called over, "You can rent fire-protection gear in the hotel lobby."

A man asked me in a low voice, "Where can I go to find men?"

"Anywhere," I replied.

"And where can I find women?" he continued.

"Uh, anywhere."

Geez, was this guy kidding? Vegas was a Super Wal-Mart of women. Thousands of party women lived there, and thousands more came from out of town to party. Vegas had more women than slot machines, in every shape, size, color, and height. All he had to do was look around. Or ask any cabbie where to go. Or pick up the phone and ask the operator for assistance.

"Can we drink in the cab?"

"Yes, but most drivers won't serve you."

D-man strolled over to me and said out of the side of his mouth, "You're not checking the First National Backseat Bank."

"The what?"

He smirked. "Does someone have to teach you how to wipe your ass, too, Rankin? Listen, when someone climbs out of the back seat, look around real quick. You'll find money, sometimes lotsa money. Bills and chips'll fall out of the fare's pocket when he pays the driver. Or sometimes the passenger doesn't shove his money deep enough in his pocket. Either way . . ." He shrugged. "Now if the driver sees the bills, they're his—everything in the cab legally belongs to him. But if you can scoop up the dough without the driver noticing . . ." D-man rubbed his thumb and index finger together, then strolled away.

I turned back to the cab line and tried to whistle for the next guy in line, but I wasn't very good at it. I put my lips together and blew, but I sprayed spit all over the man. I apologized repeatedly, but he gave me a dirty look instead of a tip.

"Here, man," T-bone said, laughing.

I looked over, and he was holding a black plastic whistle out to me. "Spitting on people ain't gonna get you tips."

"Nah, thanks," I said distastefully. "I'll buy my own. Tomorrow."

"Pardon me, sir, but is this cab safe?"

"Yes, ma'am, if the driver remembered to take his antidepressants."

A teenager looked at me with pity. "Dude, did the hotel make you buy that uniform?"

"It was free, but the humiliation of wearing it has been very costly."

He laughed appreciatively and nodded.

Okay, I told myself. It's going to be okay.

The spec house was coming together beautifully, and Cassy's stormy mood had lifted since burying Caesar several days before. She was scheduled to start her new job the next Monday, selling high-end cosmetics in a classy department store. That was a dream come true for her. It was what she wanted because she could sell anything.

Miraculously we had the same days off, but we wouldn't see each other until then. I had no idea how we'd work that out, or the money thing. I wasn't making as much in tips as predicted, and I was in this only for the money. The Grand was unbelievably busy, and I was trying to do a good job, but the guests would not tip me as consistently as they did some of the other guys.

I decided to talk to the other doormen about this. After all, we were connected as a group. After the hotel opened, security stuck together with security, waiters with waiters, dealers with dealers, bellmen with bellmen. They walked, ate, and socialized together.

When I brought up my problem in the employee cafeteria to a half-dozen of the guys, Weasel immediately offered to watch me work and offer advice. I was surprised by his sly smile . . . until the Professor quietly pointed out I'd given Weasel, the jerk he was, the opportunity to criticize me in public. Shit.

We walked out to the porte cochere and the moment of truth.

"I know you don't know what you're doing yet," Weasel announced to me in front of a hundred people, "but you've got to put on a show, move around when you call up a cab. The guests love it."

I didn't like his supercilious attitude, but I had to let it go. Maybe I would learn something from the asshole.

He lowered his voice. "When you're not getting tips, do this trick I invented. I'm real good at it. Now watch." He slid a dollar bill from his wallet into the palm of his hand.

I stepped back and watched him work the crowd. He started waving the dollar around as he put people into a taxi. "Thank you!" he yelled, and displayed the bill to the onlookers. "I appreciate that!" He pretended to tuck the buck into his pocket but instead hid it in his hand and repeated the performance.

I could see people in the taxi line digging into their pockets and purses. All of a sudden everyone was handing Weasel a tip! He took the money and looked at me smugly.

A few minutes later he swaggered over to me. "Get back to work. I can't stand around all day and teach you everything."

He walked off, leaving me with the taste of blood in my mouth.

I started to use Weasel's techniques immediately, and they worked for me, every time. Over the next several weeks I observed the other doormen carefully and noticed the nuances of opening doors for people. This job was more complex than I had thought. None of this flamboyance had been mentioned in Sharkey's curriculum because adding panache to opening doors was about making money, not maintaining control.

From Day One T-bone had used fancy dance steps to dazzle the guests, but I had mistaken them as symptoms of his hyperactivity. Now I understood it was about putting on a show. I needed to develop a style, too, but in no way was I a dancer. I had never taken dance lessons. Sure, I had danced with my wife in clubs, and I could take a turn with my mother at a family wedding. I could hardly fox trot a guest to his cab and expect to earn a reward for it.

I gamely tried spinning around to call cabs. After about fifteen minutes of this, my breath came fast and shallow, and I thought I might puke from dizziness. So what would fit my style and training? I had taken years of classes in the martial arts and boxing. My movements were swift, sharp, and strong, and I felt in balance and grounded while performing. This would be my shtick. I created unique arm movements and hand gestures based on karate and slowly attracted the crowd's attention. I kicked, I jumped. I crouched, I leapt. It paid off.

Guest ambassador? Fuck that. I was a guest sensei! People pulled out dollar bills. I don't know: maybe they thought I'd crush their Adam's apple with a quick chop if they stiffed me. Maybe it wasn't really a gratuity but protection money. Either way, I began to relax a little. I joked around more with some of the guests. The laughter helped to ease my tension.

I was in a pretty good mood. I realized I was quite taken with the job and the place. I was beginning to make more money. I mean, a *lot* more money. Was it just beginner's luck? No. Each day it just kept coming and coming and coming.

"Hey, Jay, you're really doing great out there!"

"Thanks, Dick." He had been a bellman at another hotel before the Grand opened, and he was my captain half the time I was on duty.

"I second that," the Professor said.

I had just come into the locker room to get ready for my shift before I had dinner in the cafeteria. The Professor was in his tan chinos and bare-chested, his sparse hair still wet from the shower, and Dick was sitting on a wooden bench, just hanging out. Beside him was his clipboard with our master schedule.

I really liked both these guys. The Professor had made a hobby of Las Vegas history, and during training, he had educated us with amazing stories about the city's people.

From the first day of training, Dick and I had an easygoing, laid-back relationship. He was a patient, mild man—the sort who excelled at paperwork—and I was happy to be assigned to his team. As cool a tool as he was, I would have expected Dick's eyes to be half closed and heavy lidded. Instead they bulged as if he were terrified.

Of what? I wondered. I also wondered if I should be terrified, too, and just didn't realize it yet.

Nah, I was just booby-trapping myself. In all the hotels, having a friend in management was a big deal. For me, it made all the difference in how I felt about my job. Sharkey's hostile style of supervision turned my station under the porte cochere into the OK Corral, and I was the dude without a gun. Dick, on the other hand, stood up for his crew, never threatened us, and was flexible enough when he made out our work schedules to accommodate special requests. Which it looked like he was doing now, for the Professor. The scheduling clipboard was in his lap.

"Am I interrupting anything?" I asked.

"We just finished," they said simultaneously.

"That was good. You guys practice that?" I joked.

A young man, a bellboy jogged in. His uniform jacket had a sizable dark stain down the front. He was quickly unbuttoning himself. "Dick! Can you get someone to cover for me? Look at this!"

The aroma hit me. "Whew! Is that cough syrup or Manischevitz wine?"

"It's that syrupy grape shit you get at convenience stores. This kid spilled it all over me, all over the carpet in the suite—"

"Aw, that's a shame," Dick said calmly, and stood, "but we don't have to curse. I'll call Housekeeping for the room and have someone stand in for you out front. Get another tunic and be outside as soon as you can."

"Thanks, Dick."

Off the captain went, and the bellboy, whipping off his jacket, rushed toward Wardrobe.

"Dick seems like a good guy," I said.

The Professor raised his eyebrows. "So it would seem," he said. "Have you heard the story about Bugsy Siegel and the carpet at the Frontier?"

"No. Tell me while I get changed."

The Professor explained that in the early 1940s, an architect named William Moore and his uncle had built a resort outside town and called it The Last Frontier. Both men had great connections in Hollywood, and when the Frontier opened, they brought in movie stars to entertain the guests.

"So he was already doing well when Bugsy Siegel started construction on the Flamingo in the mid-forties," the Professor went on. "Apparently Siegel did something to piss Moore off, and Moore stood up to him."

"To a gangster murderer?" I asked. "Was Moore brave or crazy?"

"Brave," the Professor replied immediately, and pulled a plaid shirt from his locker. "You'll understand in a second. Bugsy ordered a couple of his thugs to walk around the Frontier's hall-ways and pour acid on the carpets. Of course that ruined them."

"Oh, Jesus."

"Bugsy was sure his message was clear enough to send Moore scurrying underground. Instead Moore arranged a meeting with Bugsy."

"So was that brave or stupid?"

"Brave! Brave!" he insisted, laughing. "Bugsy brought body-guards along to intimidate Moore. But Moore's dealers were there, and they were tough enough to even things out."

"What happened?" I asked.

"Bugsy backed down. Word has it Siegel bought a new carpet for the Frontier, and he left Moore alone after that."

"That's supposed to be true?"

"Yep."

"That's amazing. He *was* brave. And stupid. 'Discretion being the better part of valor' and all that," I added.

"Ah, a Shakespeare scholar," the Professor said approvingly. "I'll see you tomorrow."

I sat alone, thinking. In my younger days, I had learned that the way to stop a bully was to stand up to him. Would I have gone into the ring with Bugsy Siegel? No fucking way. I was too discreet—or cowardly. Or not stupid enough. Anyway, I'd never have to find out. At my age, the days of being bullied were far behind me.

But how did this little side story about Bugsy relate to Dick? I wondered.

CHAPTER FIVE

"I never knew you were Jewish, Jay."

The bell captain who was also one of my supervisors strolled up to me. We were alone in the locker room.

"Yeah, Dick. I'm Jewish."

"I wouldn't have guessed. If you hadn't brought up Manischevitz wine last week . . ."

Here we go, I thought.

He walked toward me as I shrugged on my safari shirt. "Would you mind if I asked you a question?"

"Go ahead." I was used to answering questions about being a Jew, even though on a scale of one to ten, with ten being Orthodox, I'd say I was a two. I guess everyone has at least one identifying mark that is a part of who they are. Maybe being black or being overweight. Maybe being worth millions or playing the violin. What I discovered very early in life was, being a Jew made me different. I'm still not sure how or why, but it did. Sometimes it was a good thing, sometimes not so good.

But I never understood why my being Jewish seemed to always surprise people, even other Jews. And there were always stupid questions people would ask me about what it's like being Jewish. But Dick's question was a first.

"Jay, if one of your friends was about to drive his car off a cliff, what would you do?"

"Huh?"

"Let me put it to you this way: If *you* were driving toward the edge of a cliff, would you press the gas pedal to the floor?"

"No-o-o."

"Good! I'm glad to know you are not intentionally careening toward self-destruction."

He was pleased. I had absolutely no idea where this conversation was taking us, and I wasn't sure I wanted to be there when it arrived. I stuck my new whistle into my pocket. It made my job easier, but I had to remind myself not to blow it near a guest's ear. That faux pas always lost me money; when the guest was using his hand to clutch his blown-out ear, he could not reach into his pocket for a gratuity. I hurried with my buttons, inspected my teeth in a mirror, and checked my zipper on my way out the door. Dick followed at my heels.

"That's what you're doing, Jay. You're driving your life full throttle at disaster. As your friend, I want to save you before it's too late."

The words *save you* explained everything. Dick was on his pulpit. Sneaky bastard. He had appointed himself to save my soul. I'd seen him inside the hotel, with his supporters gathered around him as if they were members of his Our Lady of the MGM Grand congregation. They were the bellboys, mainly, younger, impressionable, and probably he could spare them from depraved behavior.

As for me, I wasn't that rah-rah about my own spiritual roots, let alone joining someone else's team. Did I ever talk to God? Did I observe traditions and rituals? Had I lost sight of who I am or where I came from? The answer to those questions was private. They belonged to me and were not, as far as I was concerned, open for discussion with anyone, including my zealous born-again supervisor. I also had to keep my anger in check. I knew myself enough to know that my explosive temper was one of my faults. I began to see that this job and the people that came with it might test my threshold.

Even though I was getting uncomfortable I didn't want to offend Dick. I took long strides toward my workstation and did not make eye contact as he continued his rant.

If I could get outside, the demands of my job would terminate his sermon.

"Jay, if you would accept Jesus Christ as your savior—"

Whoa. Dick was way out of line. He was crossing a personal boundary, violating hotel policy, and breaking federal law. It's not easy to score a hat trick with a single sentence, but he managed.

I was pissed that he had stuck me in this situation. The last thing I wanted to do was critique my supervisor's deportment, but if I did not make my feelings clear now, he'd make me his personal crusade.

I stopped in the lobby, turned, and looked him in the eyes. "Dick," I said firmly, "if this is about accepting Jesus as my savior before I drive my life off a cliff, then here's my answer to your question: I would floor the gas pedal."

With that, I was out the door, with Dick at my heels. As luck would have it, a drunk was lying flat on his back not twelve inches beyond the lobby entrance. I managed not to trip over him.

He squinted up at me from the sidewalk. "What time doesh the volcano exsh-plode?" he asked.

Dick rushed over to hoist the lush to his feet so I quick-stepped to my station. The area was mobbed with guests, and T-bone was happy to see me. I recognized an elderly, blue-haired lady at the head of the taxi line. She was a casino regular. I whistled a cab up for her and opened the back door. Now, like every other time she left the hotel, she asked me sweetly, "Will the taxi bring me back here?"

"Of course," I assured her. "But you have to leave first."

"Oh, you and your jokes!" she said appreciatively, and poked me in the arm.

I liked old Blue Hair. I hoped Vegas would be good to her.

The next person in line stepped to the front. "Can you tell me if the games are fixed?"

"I didn't know they were broken," I replied, and helped him into the cab.

The next man grabbed my attention, looked me straight in the eyes, and pleaded, "Can you get me some topless-show tickets?"

"Sure. No problem." T-bone and I always carried various comp passes to some of the clubs. We gave them to any guest who asked.

I sneaked a look at Dick. He and someone from Security were half-carrying the drunk into the lobby. I hoped my lack of interest in the discussion would dissuade him from proselytizing, but I probably didn't stand a chance in hell of that. I couldn't worry about that now; everything was too hectic. I put Dick out of my mind and decided to steer clear of any and all bosses.

Soon I found my rhythm. I felt the adrenaline surging through my body. A sense of energy permeated my being. I was lucky, selected from so many thousands of applicants. Personnel had chosen me to stand in the cool night air at the entrance to a world-class resort. I was having a good time, putting on my show, and using my instincts with humor to make people laugh.

Being a doorman was more exciting than I ever could have guessed. It was like being out on the street, or at Times Square on New Year's Eve—the drunks, hookers, winners, and losers against the backdrop of laughter and flashing lights. Life shone with a blinding, pulsing beauty. It was all there before me, to work with, to get to know, to become a part of.

Maybe this is who I am, after all. I realized. I started up a routine as if I were a late-night talk-show announcer. "Ladeeze and gennulmen, heeerrre's a high roller! Feast your eyes on those jewels!"

My arms became windmills. I spun on one foot and then went for the door of a cab. As I yanked it open, I kicked my leg high, karate-style.

The crowd applauded every gesture and laughed at every comment I made. They reached into pocket and purse to thrust dollar bills at me. As I stuffed the money into my pockets, I felt vindicated: I had taken a leap in faith that Cassy and I would be solvent even if she quit Caesar's, and now, with my pockets bulging, I knew I had been right. This wasn't beginner's luck, either; I was getting good at what I did. I would in time be fuckin' great as a doorman.

D-man's advice about inspecting the backseat of taxis had proved extremely lucrative. T-bone and I found money—bills, change, and chips—and cameras, jewelry, purses. To cash in, we had to be fast, very fast, and we were. I would open the cab door for a guest, see the money, and snatch the loot with the speed of a snake. Sometimes the cab driver would turn around, but he was always too late to claim the booty.

If a cabbie ever challenged me, I would say I was merely getting rid of some trash from the seat, and then I would go through the motions of wiping it off as I hid the stash from his line of vision.

Yeah, Cassy and I would do just fine financially. My job would never fade away because some people will always want to gamble. I'd never been too attracted to it myself, but playing slot machines had been a craze on the Left Coast since the late 1800s. By the early 1900s, you could find slot machines in Las Vegas bars. You could also play the one-armed bandit when you waited for a haircut, while you drank a cup of coffee, as you bought yourself some smokes.

Men couldn't get enough of any newfangled machinery, and that included the games with gears that spewed coins on the basis of dumb luck. Didn't matter if you were smart, skillful, or deserving. You just had to show up at the right time at the right machine and play for a while. Every time you thought about calling it a night, you stayed put. You just knew the next guy to come along would pull that lever and take home the dough that by rights belonged in *your* pocket.

Even my biological dad had a slot machine, against the wall in his used-furniture store in Vegas. He let me play it when I visited him that one time. It cost a nickel to play, and I loved it. Every time I ran out of money, he would unlock the slot door and scoop out a handful of coins so I could keep playing.

Almost everyone in America knew Nevada was the first state to legalize casino-style gambling. Few realize that Nevada outlawed gaming in 1910 with a law so rigid, two buddies couldn't even flip a coin to decide who got to introduce himself to the redhead sitting alone at the bar. The Nevada Legislature didn't approve a legalized gambling bill until a few years later. The unlikely sponsor was some rancher, named Tobin, who never set foot in Las Vegas and had zero interest in gambling.

Of course between 1910 and 1931 plenty of illegal gaming houses operated, similar to speakeasies during Prohibition.

If a gambler or a drinker is going to quit, it's going to be on his own terms. Every year the number of gamblers increased. Yeah, Cassy and I would be fine.

"You know what's funny?" I asked my wife when we bumped into each other a few days later. Now that she had begun her new job, we usually weren't awake at the same time. "I was never totally sold on the idea of being a doorman. I went ahead with my application only because the money was supposed to be so great. Now I'm really taken with the place and the job."

"That's nice, honey." Cassy was dressed in a crisp white blouse with pearl buttons and a slim navy skirt that skimmed the top of her knees. She caught her thick dark hair in a navy ribbon at the nape of her neck. Her fashion statement had swung from resort raunchy toward the tasteful conservatism favored by high-end department stores.

I followed her from the bathroom to her walk-in closet, where she slipped on navy pumps with two-inch chunky heels. "I mean, anyone who lives in Las Vegas knows that other than management, the most prestigious job in town is being the doorman at a big, expensive hotel. It's a position that seems to be respected by everyone in the industry."

"And your hotel is the biggest." She smiled at me as she brushed past on the way to the kitchen.

"Right. And the doorman is the face of that hotel—the first person the guests see upon arrival and the last one they see when they're leaving. We get people what they want. I wouldn't want to work anywhere else in the hotel than right out in front."

"I'm so proud of you, honey, that it's working out so well."

I admired her ass as she stuck her head into the refrigerator and burrowed around for her lunch.

"T-bone told me that fourteen hundred guys applied for the doorman jobs."

"Imagine that!" She came up for air with a small container of yogurt and an apple.

I didn't want to start a fight before my wife went to work, but if I didn't say something, I'd brood all day. "Cas . . ."

"Hmm?"

"You seem, I don't know, distracted. Are our schedules okay for you? Are you just preoccupied with getting ready for work, or do we need to talk later?"

She slammed the refrigerator door and wheeled on me. All the distant pleasantness had vanished. "Oh? You mean we might actually be able to talk later?" she asked sarcastically.

Jesus. What had I walked into? "If you want to. If you do, I do. You know that."

Her green eyes blazed. "Just how am I supposed to know that if I never see you, Jay? You're working, or I'm working. You're out, and I'm at home. I'm at work, and you're here. I want to be like normal married people." She made a noise in her throat, almost a growl, of anger and frustration.

"I won't quit my job," I said. "Do you want to leave yours and go back to working nights?"

"No! Work is the only time I'm happy. We don't have any fun anymore. You used to be fun. You used to be funny. We used to have a good time together. Now we've got nothing! I want to go out, but you're always too tired!"

She was sobbing and trying to salvage her mascara. I grabbed a paper towel off the counter and held it toward her, but she batted it away. "Who are you funny for, Jay? It sure isn't me. If I gave you a dollar to stick in your pocket, would you be funny for me? Huh? Would you dance and kick for me?"

"Oh, Cas—" I tried to gather her in my arms, but she shoved me away with so much force, I was shocked.

"Oh, go fuck yourself!" she screamed. Her yogurt slipped from her grasp and exploded on the floor, spraying her shoes and stockings with white goop in strawberry sauce. "Fuck!" she shrieked, and hurled her apple at the wall. "Fuck! Look what you made me do!" She snatched a dishtowel from the counter and ran out the door.

After cleaning up the mess I stood in the kitchen for a while, doing nothing, my mind blank. My life had come to a full stop. I thought we were on the edge of having it all. The pieces had come together, I thought. Both of us had jobs we liked, and the spec house moving ahead of schedule.

I had to acknowledge, though, that Cassy had a point. I'd tell her that when she came home. We'd try to figure things out.

Working in a Las Vegas hotel nullified the Monday-through-Friday/nine-to-five order of the universe. After only a few weeks on the job, I no longer operated with a normal concept of time. My work schedule had Cassy and me both fucked, and I wondered if we would ever adjust to it—or ever want to. My dinner break was at eleven at night, for God's sake. Who in their right mind eats dinner at eleven? I was ready to go *home* at eleven, not break for dinner. But I'd have to work till 3 AM, all for another fifty, seventy-five, hundred bucks in tips.

In a larger sense, I had begun to lose track of the days. I was not the only one, either: Within the hotel, I heard coworkers say, "Today is my Monday," or "This is my Friday."

Outside Las Vegas, the workweek began with Monday and ended with Friday. But Saturday was my Monday. Which meant Monday was my hump day, Wednesday was my Friday, and Thursday and Friday were my weekend. I couldn't find anyone to party with on my Saturday night because it was Thursday, which was their Monday or Tuesday. Monday Night Football was played on my Wednesday.

Worse, my shift "swung," which completely turned my life inside out. If I wanted to socialize with someone who worked days, we would have to meet at three in the morning.

Obviously I hadn't gone to the gym with Sam recently. T-bone and I had started working out together, though, and once I learned to ignore his motor mouth, I liked being with him. He knew so much about weight training, he suggested slight adjustments to my technique, and already I could feel the benefits.

Not all adaptations had been that easy. My normal routines were so twisted around, a couple of times I couldn't figure out why the sky was dark with stars instead of light blue with the sunshine. I became confused about when to eat, go to the bathroom, or check the mail. My body battled against the upheaval with the same tenacity it would muster to reject a mismatched organ transplant. My thirst seemed unquenchable, and I was chronically constipated. I needed Valium.

Cassy and I had not blown off steam for a long time. Sometimes I missed the days of hard-driven fun with my crazy, great pack of buddies—"the dogs," we called ourselves. We danced, drank, laughed, and let go.

So my bizarre schedule was tough on both of us. Cassy and I were in such complete agreement; I couldn't believe we were arguing about it. She complained she never saw me, and I always wanted to come home to her. My idea of nirvana was curling up on the sofa with Cassy and watching a good movie on television. I fantasized about little else during the final four hours of my shift: coming home from work and taking a shower. (The stench of exhaust fumes, cigars, and money clung to my uniform, my hair, and my skin. Sometimes I felt as if the chemicals had permeated my body, and the smell was emanating from inside my guts.) Cleansed, I would sit on the sofa with Cas, elevate my swollen feet, and eat as much as I could to balance out the amount of calories I burned at my job.

It was a perfect vision. In real life, though, Cassy wanted to go out. Since the first week of our conflicting schedules, we'd been over this again and again with no resolution. She wanted to party with me on Thursdays and have a good time after my shift. I was too tired from the stress and physical exertion at the core of my job. I needed to rest. I had no choice; I felt as if I had been beaten with a club.

"Let's go out on tomorrow night," I would suggest, "after I've had a chance to recuperate."

"I don't want to go out on Fridays," she would tell me. "I have to work Saturday mornings."

We won't have that argument again, I vowed now. I had to keep her happy, whatever the cost. I would not place our marriage at risk. *Divorce* and *Las Vegas* had been said in the same breath since the early days, when the Nevada legislature loosened the requirements for residency. The law allowed people to extricate themselves from an unhappy marriage in as few as six weeks. Word about it got around fast, as the wealthy and the well known took advantage of the service.

Soon an entire industry sprang up around the so-called quickie divorce. The seekers, mostly women, relaxed at dude ranches while they qualified for resident status and then completed the legalities.

I wasn't being judgmental about how fast and convenient divorce had become. In many ways the system had been a good thing: These ranches set the stage for the huge, rambling resorts that eventually were to replace them along the Strip, and many miserable people desperately needed their freedom. But Cassy and I were going to take a different tack. We were going to make this thing work, or I'd die trying.

"Do you partake in anything?"

I turned around. T-bone and I were standing under the porte cochere a couple of nights after Cassy's blowup. The temperature had plunged into the thirties, so we were having a slow shift with plenty of time to hang out. T-bone was waiting for a reply, but I had no idea what the hell he was asking me. "Do I what?"

"You know. Partake." He gestured in a way that back east meant, C'mon, c'mon, c'mon. Ya thick or somethin'?

Suddenly I realized what he was asking, and I had to laugh. "Shit, T-bone, I didn't mean to be so dense. Yeah, I 'partake.' I like to feel good and take a break from my life."

He nodded happily. "I have painkillers if you ever need them."

"Thanks, man."

"Anytime."

He jogged off as a taxi pulled up.

I was honored. His wasn't an offer merely to get high. This was T-bone's way of telling me we were building trust. Confiding in a colleague about recreational drug use was a big deal at the Grand—a big deal in any hotel in town. If a supervisor learned that an employee was taking drugs just to get high, he would dismiss that employee at the speed of light.

Supervisors were proactive about maintaining a drug-free staff, and corporate procedures closed any possible loopholes. Before the hotel opened we applicants were expected to submit to a drug test as part of the Grand's hiring process. Once hired, though, we were obligated by the terms of our employment to urinate on demand at other times, too.

Now, looking at T-bone opening the cab's back door, I felt optimistic about our friendship—almost a complete turnaround from my initial attitude toward him.

I noticed T-bone was limping slightly, and he had one hand pressed to his lower back.

"You okay?" I asked.

"Fine," he said. "Listen. Maybe you and your wife would like to go out with me and Mary sometime. You know, have a couple of drinks, a few laughs."

"That would be great," I said sincerely. "I'd like to meet Mary, and Cassy's been, uh, wanting socialize more. I promised her we would."

T-bone gave me a knowing smile. "I'll have Mary call her, okay? They can figure it out." He paused. "You like reggae, by any chance?"

Perfect. "Yeah, T-bone," I said with a straight face. "I partake in reggae."

CHAPTER SIX

On the first night of my visit, my biological dad, whose name was Ben, introduced me to the fine art of tipping. He led me into the casino at Caesar's Palace, an astonishing world unlike any I could have imagined. I was swept up by the sights and sounds, the beauty and excitement.

Ben seemed to know everyone working there—the pit bosses, the hosts, and the bell captains all knew him by name. Everyone was so nice to us. I observed his behavior carefully and tucked away his example of how "someone with class" interacts with everyone inside a casino.

Coming from a household strapped for cash, I wondered if my estranged father might have been going overboard with his generosity. But his tipping obviously gave him happiness, made me feel important, and pleased the recipient, so it was, I decided, a good use of disposable income. As an eleven-year-old, I didn't suspect he might be a big gambler and that staying on good terms with the casino staff often resulted in free meals or some other comp. That night I could only believe that this guy who called me son was king of the city, and I was his crown prince.

Then, suddenly, he was nearly dethroned. A security guard intercepted us and blocked our way. "You can't bring a child in here," he said, and frowned down at me. "It's against the law. You'll have to take him out of the casino."

I held my breath. I didn't like that I was a problem, and I didn't want to leave the casino. Ben was a stranger to me, so I had no idea if he would hustle me out the door or, instead, argue with the guard. I was nervous because back home I had heard stories about how violent he could become.

I watched as he smoothly drew some bills from his pocket and discreetly pressed them into the guard's palm. "I'm taking the kid to dinner," he explained in a reasonable tone, and he nodded toward a restaurant at the back of the casino.

For a moment the guard said nothing. Then he stood aside and assumed a deferential posture. "That's all right, then. If you're just passing through."

Then the guard held the bills out to Ben. "This isn't necessary . . ."

"It's okay. You've been nice to my boy. I appreciate that."

"Thank you, sir."

The guard ruffled my hair, which I endured, and then Ben and I continued into the heart of the casino.

Rather than being deposed, I felt the increased power and stability of his monarchy.

Throughout the night, people came over to us just to say hello to Ben, and he introduced me to them. All his friends seemed to have the identical first name: Tony. This scenario repeated throughout my brief stay in Las Vegas.

"I want you to shake hands with a friend of mine," Ben told me at the end of the evening. He guided me toward a black man sitting in a wheelchair in the lobby.

"Joe," he said, "I'd like to present my son to you. He's visiting from Los Angeles."

I held out my hand, and Joe grasped it firmly. "Hey—Daddy showin' you a good time?"

"Yessir," I said, "and we still have two more days!"

Joe chuckled. "Well, you two enjoy yourseffs."

"We will!" I promised, and Ben ushered me toward the door as several people came to pay homage to the man in the wheelchair.

"That was Joe Louis, Jay," my father said. "He's the most famous light-heavyweight boxer of all time."

"Wow," I said. "Joe Louis."

I don't recall that we ever went to a restaurant or had dinner, but I was too happy to be hungry. I climbed into Ben's car, and as we drove to pick up his beautiful girlfriend at the Frontier, I studied his profile, thrown in high relief by the flashing neon signs. I was in awe of his kingdom—the casino's sounds, lights, and smells made me feel as if I had traveled to a magical planet.

Maybe that was why I had come back to Vegas. This was the place where I had felt important and connected. I had never felt that way before. I had been searching for it ever since.

So all these years later, when the Weasel issued his warning about my connecting with people and building a network of friends, I was blindsided. We sat by ourselves at a table in the cafeteria a few days after the incident with Bug-Eyed Dick.

"Looks like you and your partner are getting pretty chummy," the Weasel said, and peeled back the top slice of white bread so he could inspect the sandwich filling. He raked some raw onion slices onto his tray.

"Yeah, we work really well together," I told him. "We're trying out some ideas to move the cab line along faster, and he suggested we—"

"Never socialize with coworkers," the Weasel told me, removing a thick tomato slice and a nest of fresh alfalfa sprouts. "Jesus Christ, look at this shit, will ya? What's the cook thinking?" When he removed the lettuce and pesto mayonnaise so all that remained was turkey on white bread, he seemed satisfied. "I don't make friends at work. Never have. It's my policy."

The Weasel ripped an aggressive bite from his dinner.

I tried not to watch him eat. He went after his food as if he were competing against it.

"Actually our wives—"

"Don't trust anyone, Rankin. Not just here. At any hotel. Everyone's your enemy. The sooner you get that, the safer your job'll be."

"Even you?" I asked, smiling.

"Even me," he shot back. He held my gaze and seemed completely serious.

"I don't know, man," I said. "I don't want to live like that. I believe most people have good intentions toward—"

The Weasel snorted with derision. "That's real sweet, Jay," he said sarcastically. "But it ain't life."

"I—"

"You're fucked, is what you are," he said. "I'm telling you to hold everyone, T-bone especially, at a distance. Everything you say that isn't strictly business gets repeated and distorted. By the time some scumbag carries it to management's ears—and I promise you, this *will* happen—it's all twisted and costing you your job. But, hey, don't take my word for it. You'll find out for yourself."

Three other men sat down with us, so the Weasel finally shut his mouth. I ate as quickly as I could, then headed for my station. Walking along the hallway and up the stairs, I mulled over what the Weasel had said, and then I decided to disregard it. I'd seen plenty of employees hanging out together at work, joking around, having a good time. The Weasel was one of the few employees I could think of who looked bitter and alienated. He wouldn't have to worry about my trying to be friends with him. He wasn't my type.

Friendships were important to me. I never saw Sam anymore, and T-bone and I worked like a team of two horses. The Weasel was just an asshole, the last person I should trust for advice. As my grad-school adviser would have said, the Weasel's so-called policy was more likely a post-hoc rationalization for his not having any friends. Yeah.

I climbed the stairs two at a time to the lobby level and looked forward to getting better acquainted with the cab drivers. Sometimes they kept me company. The cold weather would make for a slow night, so we'd have time to shoot the shit.

I walked outside, and my breath formed clouds of condensation around my face. At the driveway, T-bone was a blur of energy and enthusiasm, his breath coming fast in white puffs. No fucking way could he seem so genuine and, simultaneously, pose a threat.

At two in the morning, after my partner had clocked out and gone home, I paced under the porte cochere, trying to keep warm. The weather exhausted me. Trying to stay warm drained all my energy, and boredom slowed the time left on my shift. Most people were inside the hotel having a good time.

The cabs were lined up in their queue, but I doubted the drivers would have many more fares. On cold and quiet nights like this, a cabbie would occasionally drive up from the queue to where I was standing, just to let me warm my frozen hands over the vehicle's heating vents. Piccolo Pete was there for me many times this way. Sometimes the wind-chill factor was so extreme,

I would open Pete's passenger door and use it as a shield against the frigid gusts.

In nicer weather, when hotel traffic was busy, Pete would drive up so I could grab on to his door handle and lean back, bending from the waist, my butt sticking way out, to stretch my tight and aching back and shoulders.

I wondered if he was still waiting his turn in the extremely long line of idling taxis or if he had gone home after his last fare.

All the hotels in Vegas had to be slow because of the weather, so the drivers stayed put. Some of them were standing in a tight circle, talking in the driveway. I watched a taxi pull out of the line, and its flashing headlights created a haloed silhouette of the men quick-stepping from its path. I recognized Piccolo Pete as he rolled to a stop beside me under the porte cochere. He leaned to open the passenger door, and I jumped inside.

"Thanks, man," I told him. "All I want to do is go home and take a hot shower. My feet are numb."

"I don't know how you can take it," he said, "standing for hours in weather like this."

"Who told you I *can*?" I asked. "I hate the cold. I'm fucking miserable."

"I hear ya." Pete reached down to the floor between his legs and mine and brought out a small black case. "Maybe this will get the blood flowing."

I watched with interest as he opened the lid, withdrew a clarinet, and fit the pieces together.

"How long you been playing?" I asked.

"Jesus. Forty years? Hard to believe."

"Professionally?"

He laughed, sort of, and his eyes shone. "Being a musician doesn't pay the bills, so let's say I drive a cab professionally."

I smiled, and we both climbed from his car. Pete leaned against the side of his cab, licked his lips, and then brought the instrument to his mouth.

I listened, watching him play while the stiff wind lifted a shock of hair from his forehead, then set it back down.

The cabbies loosened their huddle and turned to listen. One, Sweet Caroline, approached us. Her gait was fluid, slow, sexy. All hips and shoulders. She leaned next to Pete and accompanied him with an incredible, soulful voice.

Don't know why there's no sun up in the sky
Stormy weather
Since my man and I ain't together,
keeps rainin' all the time.

Life is bare, gloom and mis'ry everywhere
Stormy weather
Just can't get my poor self together,
I'm weary all the time . . .

I stood, transfixed, as they performed under the Las Vegas stars. It was, bar none, the best performance in town. I know a transcendent moment when I see one, and I thought, it doesn't get any better than this, right here and right now.

Then, surprisingly, it did get better: Sam pulled up in a limousine and joined us, and I felt even happier, sharing the experience with one of my best buds. His presence banished the loneliness and emptiness I often suffered once T-bone clocked out.

Sam and Caroline made some pretty heated eye contact as she sang, "'Don't be a naughty baby, come to Mama, come to Mama do-o-o-o. My sweet embraceable you . . .'"

Oh, shit, I thought.

After a couple more numbers, Pete and Caroline ended their set to resounding applause and hooting. I quickly blocked Sam's path to Caroline, gripped his arm firmly, and led him away.

"Good to see you, man!" I said. He was looking over his shoulder at her. "What the fuck are you doing, driving a limo?"

"New job," he told me. "Fits better with my training schedule than construction." He stopped and looked around at our surroundings. "This place is un-fucking-believable, Jay. How about you getting me a job here?"

"Oh, sure, man, since I carry so much fucking weight with the management. In fact, why don't I just call them right now, wake 'em up, and tell 'em to get down here with a set of keys for my man Sam?"

"Asshole," Sam said, laughing.

I loved being with him. All we did was laugh. It was great. When he was around, I felt totally relaxed, like every jittery cell in my body was taking a breather. Somehow Sam's laid-back attitude tranquilized me. His gait was a leisurely swagger, so I had to slow my pace significantly to stay in step with him. Probably something as simple as that accounted for my feeling so good in his company.

"No, seriously. What kind of work do you have in mind?"

"I like what I'm doing now, but working for a gypsy limo company is too iffy for me. Could you try to get me a position as a chauffeur with a limo service sanctioned by the Grand?"

"I'll see what I can do as soon as I can." I promised. I doubted I'd find him anything. Sam was an impressive guy, but I didn't have any connections other than periodically schmoozing with one of the limo managers of the hotel. "So you like the driving?"

He lowered his voice, although we were alone. "This evening, these two gorgeous women get into the back seat. I ask where they want me to take them—which, in retrospect, is what I should say to everyone—and they say they want me to take them to heaven. I laugh at their joke, then I can see they're not being funny. They fuckin' invite me to get into the back with them, so I can take them to heaven!"

"Jesus, Sam. So what did you do?"

He gave me the "duh" look. I half-expected him to do T-bone's c'mon-c'mon hand roll. *Am* I an idiot? I wondered, and remembered all the shit the Weasel had shoveled on me just a few hours before.

I had never thought of myself as being naive. Did I just have to adjust to new rules? I was used to the behavior of California, which was deceptive and loose enough. Las Vegas was nothing like Cal—or anywhere else in the universe, so far as I could tell.

". . . not identical twins but still un-fucking-believable, man," Sam was saying. "So the tall one, she . . ."

I drifted back to my thoughts. I didn't give a shit about the tall one—or the short one, either. I wanted to hear about Sam's wife. I considered Sheila to be a good woman deserving of his fidelity. I wanted to know how their daughter, one of the world's cutest infants, was enjoying life on planet Earth. This particular moment didn't seem like the optimum time to inquire about them. That, or the timing couldn't have been better. I couldn't even tell anymore.

I hated being so opinionated. If I didn't get a handle on my judgments, our friendship would go sour, and that was the last thing I wanted. Friends like Sam were almost impossible to find. Unless he had changed drastically from the man I thought he was. I decided I would think about this more when I wasn't so cold and tired and hungry.

". . . go up to Stevie Wonder's room," Sam continued, "and he introduces me to his wife. I spent the entire night there, talking to Stevie and his friends. We had such a great time, he asked me to come back the next night, and we've been buddies ever since." Sam stopped and took a breath, studying me. "But I've probably told you that story already."

"Uh, no, Sam. You haven't." I was a little pissed, and I couldn't understand why. "You've never told me that you even *knew* Stevie Wonder."

"Yeah, well, I do. Last week Stevie wanted to go out at two in the morning and find a music store. He calls me to take him and his crew. When we get there, I find out he had already invited some other musicians, and they jammed all fuckin' night. It was incredible, man. They played nonstop until six in the morning. I couldn't believe how—"

I heard a squawk, and Sam dug a mobile phone with walkie-talkie capabilities from his pocket. The dispatcher told him he had a fare at Mandalay Bay.

Sam returned the phone to his pocket. "Gotta go, man. Great seeing you, buddy." He gave me a bear hug and thumped me on the back. "Don't be a stranger."

I watched him get into his limo and drive away. I was relieved Caroline had already gone.

I took a deep, cold breath and went inside to warm up, clock out, and shake off my mood. Why was I so pissed? It had to be connected to Sam's stupid story about Stevie Wonder and the other stupid bullshit story about screwing the twins in the back seat of the limo. No fucking way could he have kept a friendship with Stevie Wonder a secret from me; we spent too much time together for it not to have slipped into conversation. He would have *had* to make *some* reference to it. He wouldn't keep secrets from me, anyway, I thought. No way!

Okay, I decided. Both stories had to be complete, utter, and absolute crap. Now I got pissed at myself for being so angry with Sam for fooling around on Sheila, when obviously that had never happened.

I am one fucking moron, I decided, shaking my head and laughing. He really had me going, the fucker. Feeling much better, I turned toward the Transportation department to find the comedian a job.

"Rankin!"

I turned to see Sharkey and another captain, with whom I never had much contact, hurrying down the corridor toward me. Sharkey glanced at the Transportation office door and then raised his eyebrows at me.

"What were you doing there, Rankin?" he asked.

I was going to tell him it was none of his fucking business, but as one of my supervisors, he had a right to know if I was requesting a transfer. "One of my friends wants to drive a limo." I shrugged as if to say, no big deal.

Sharkey nodded, apparently satisfied. "We want you to talk to the other doormen for us." He indicated to the other captain, who stood ramrod straight, his chin tucked, his eyes burning with rage.

"All right . . ." I said warily.

"Last weekend was a disgrace," Sharkey told me, and stabbed his finger at me. "You tell the doormen that they'd better get their shit together, and I mean immediately, or the whole damned lot of you will be out of a job."

I stared at him. "It was pretty chaotic," I agreed, "but isn't Christmas and the holidays always a different—"

"He didn't ask for a debate," the other captain said sharply. "Tell the others. We will fire all of you if you guys don't get it together. You'd best be worrying about your own job before trying to bring your friends onboard."

CHAPTER SEVEN

The revelers at Reggae Madness were packed so tight on the dance floor, they created a seemingly impenetrable, pulsating wall. T-bone looked at me, eyebrows raised. Our wives stood between us; our table awaited us on the far side of the nightclub.

"Hey, you were the marine," I shouted to him.

"But I wasn't a landing-support specialist," he yelled back, and the four of us laughed.

"No one's gonna try to stop you, Todd," Mary said.

She had a point. He was wearing a tight silk T-shirt that displayed his muscular arms, shoulders, and chest.

"Unless they're crazy," Cassy said. "And so far I haven't noticed anyone here who could pass for normal."

"Lead on, grunt!" I urged, and hoped Cassy's sarcastic remark was an anomaly. I couldn't remember how many shots she had knocked back while we waited for the table.

"Follow me, troops!" he roared, and he took Mary's hands and placed them on his hips.

We fell in behind them, single file, with Cassy's hands at Mary's waist, and mine at Cassy's. T-bone's strategy was to become part of the energy and the rhythm and samba our way to our table. As I brought up the rear, I watched men turn to stare at my decked-out wife.

She had on a new dress—her first department-store purchase using her employee discount perk—and it was a deep green, formfitting stunner. Crystal beads woven into gold netting adorned the bodice, and when these caught the dance floor's spotlights, tiny rainbows sparked on my wife's breasts and shoulders.

Cassy was tall and slender and a good dancer. She would attract men's attention in any city on the planet. In Vegas, though, a dangerous fringe stalked the clubs and hunted for babes, sometimes at any cost. Women had to be careful because with these guys, things could get ugly fast.

Beautiful women like Cassy were especially vulnerable because they were accustomed to having power over men. The symmetry of their features, the silkiness of their hair, the curves of their body, had always put them in control. In Vegas, they were nothing more than targets for men who grabbed what they wanted.

But I didn't want to think about that crap now. I just wanted to have a good time. The four of us reached the far side of the dance floor and fell, laughing, into a booth. We continued to dance to the throbbing beat, even though we were seated. The band was now peaking on the intensity of a traditional reggae rhythm that made holding still impossible. The whole place was going crazy.

Cassy looked flushed and happy. She reached down and squeezed my thigh. I had promised her we would go out, and within the week, badda bing.

"Did ya hear about D-man?" T-bone asked, leaning across the table.

"What about him?" Cassy asked.

She didn't even know D-man, so T-bone got knocked off balance for a moment. Then he continued, "He found a fucking diamond ring in the back seat of a cab the other day."

"No shit!" I said.

"What'd he do with it?" Mary asked.

"When are *you* going to find a ring, Jay?" Cassy asked.

We laughed.

"He turned it into the Lost and Found," T-bone said. He looked at the girls. "That's hotel policy. We have to do that if we find something really valuable. If no one claims it within thirty days, then finders keepers."

He laughed and shook his head. "Before he'd give 'em the ring, he insisted on an appraisal from one of the lobby jewelry stores."

"That was smart," Mary said. "Otherwise how would he know he was getting back the same stone he'd found?"

"Yeah." T-bones eyes shone. "Everyone sitting down and holding on? It appraised at thirty-five thousand."

"Oh fuuuuck," I groaned.

"So stay tuned, ladies and gentleman."

We sat and watched the dancers.

"This is one of our favorite places," Mary said, leaning across the table.

A waitress with a braided ponytail appeared at our table, with glasses and a very expensive bottle of wine. "Hi, Mary," she said brightly. "Franco says you and your friends should relax and have a good time."

"Thank you, Krista," Mary said. She half stood and located the manager at the bar. She waved and mouthed *thank you,* then sat back down.

Cassy laughed. "With service like that, I can understand why you'd like this place." She held a glass out to T-bone, who was studying the label.

"Happens all the time, everywhere," he said proudly, "because of Mary being a concierge."

"Whatever works." Cassy stated, and pushed her glass forward, a little insistently, I thought. Calm the fuck down, Jay.

"Guests depend heavily on the concierge for recommendations," Mary explained.

"And Franco hopes she'll send them here," T-bone said, and poured the wine.

Cassy laughed. "Well, tell Franco that I tell my customers where to go, too, if you know what I mean." She took a swallow. "Whoa. This is good stuff!" She raised her glass. "To favors and bribes!" she said, and tried to stand and look behind us. "Thank you, Franco!"

I saw Mary and T-bone exchange a quick glance. "Here, honey, sit down." I forced a smile. "You don't even know what the guy looks like." I put my arm around Cassy's hips and moved over a bit, easing her back to the booth.

Her cat's eyes sparked. "Jesus Christ, Jay. Don't you think I worked in a nightclub long enough to be able to pick out a manager from the customers?"

"Who wants to dance?" T-bone asked frantically. "C'mon, Cassy." He was already out of the booth, holding a hand to her.

She hesitated just long enough to give me a nasty look, then reached up for his fingers. I stood and invited Mary to dance.

"If you don't mind, Jay, I'd be happy just to sit here for a while."

"No problem." I felt a little awkward as I sat down.

Mary poured me a glass of wine. "Todd talks about you all the time."

"The guy is a workhorse, Mary. We make a really good team." I hoped she could tell how much I meant it. "And he tells me all about you, too."

T-bone was fortunate to have found such a classy lady. The woman had brains. She was fluent in five languages and had worked her way up to being one of the top concierges in Las Vegas. She was devoted to him and grounded enough to be his anchor. Mary was a lot of fun, though, always up.

Like Cassy, she was pretty, but in an entirely different way. South American, she wore her black hair short and sleek, and her dark eyes and lashes looked dramatic even without cosmetics. T-bone had warned me she talked a mile a minute (so did he), but with her providing both sides of the conversation, all I had to do was sit back and listen. Then the small talk took a sudden, sullen turn.

"You and I have a lot in common," she said slowly, and her eyes slewed toward our partners on the dance floor. "Neither one of them knows when to say when."

I shifted uncomfortably and waited for her to continue.

"Todd's back is getting worse, Jay. He thinks his disks are deteriorating, and I have no reason to think he's exaggerating."

"What?"

I was taken back. I'd been to the gym several times with T-bone in the last two weeks, and he had shown no signs of discomfort. The guy was bench-pressing 250 pounds. In fact, I was nervous about spotting him by myself when he hefted all that weight.

Todd was also a great trainer. He had all these fine points to pass along about my form when I was doing free weights.

"Mary, we're hauling heavy luggage out of cabs and limos all night long!"

She shrugged as if to say, why do you think I brought this up? "Todd's back problems started when he was in the marines, then they turned chronic when he started lifting heavy weights at the gym." She made a derisive sound that had a distinctly Spanish air about it. "He was trying to strengthen his body, and instead he's caused it to implode."

"Has he had X-rays?"

She shook her head. "Not recently. He doesn't want to know."

"If he hasn't had X-rays, then how can you be sure his condition is serious? I mean, I'm sure he's dead tired when he gets home. We blow ourselves out for the entire shift. I can barely move when I get home, and I've never had a back problem. If we've been to the gym, I'm a physical wreck." I leaned forward and looked into her eyes. "I've watched him, Mary. He doesn't act like someone with a serious back problem. T-bone doesn't stop for a second. Don't you think I'd have noticed if—"

"That's why I'm telling you, Jay," she said, biting off the words with her teeth. "He doesn't want anything to jeopardize his job. He's almost anesthetized on painkillers. Otherwise he wouldn't be able to function."

Mary paused to take a sip of her wine, and she studied me over the rim of her glass. What was she trying to figure out? I found out soon enough. "He was furious when he heard Sharkey and that other captain had threatened to fire everyone. So T-bone and another doorman—I think you guys call him Weasel? He works days—took themselves straight to the top and complained."

I had the feeling my life had just derailed and was about to become twisted, smoking wreckage. "The top of what? Who'd they talk to? Why didn't he tell me?"

She shrugged nonchalantly, but Mary knew that her husband had just dropped me into a vat of shit. "I'm not sure who it was. Someone in upper management."

"Jesus fucking Christ!" I had to clutch the side of the table to keep myself from charging the dance floor and beating T-bone to a pulp. "Wait till Sharkey finds out! Oh, fuck."

"He already knows."

"What?"

"Before he left the office, he heard the boss man issue orders for Sharkey to report to his office—"

"Oh, fuck." I cradled my head in my hands. Sharkey was going to think *I* had filed the complaint, because I was the one he had told to spread word.

"-and to bring his ID and keys."

"Oh, fuck!" I was so upset, I couldn't figure out if I'd be better off if Sharkey had been fired or just called on the carpet.

"Try not to be too angry with Todd," she pleaded. "A grand delusion takes over his body when he's high on drugs. He thinks he's invincible, and he doesn't consider any consequences. He believed he was doing the right thing for everybody by reporting Sharkey."

"So what do you want me to do?" I asked, miserable.

"Just keep an eye on him. Try to get him to be careful with his back."

"Okay, I will." I, more than T-bone, would have to be careful now. His and Weasel's stunt had put my butt on the line.

"Thank you, and I'm sorry," she said, and relief washed over her features.

We fell silent, and I sipped moodily at my wine. "Mary, if he's on so many painkillers, how is he able to function at all out there? He should be a zombie."

"Coke."

"He's high on cocaine?"

She nodded. "A lot of coke."

Oh, Jesus, I thought. Here's this health nut who lectures us on fluid intake, vitamin supplements, and organic food, all while he's doing uppers and downers. Jesus fucking Christ. God, T-bone. Shit.

"If he's snorting all this coke during our shift to stay alert and pumped, how can he fall asleep when he gets home?" I braced myself for her answer.

"Vodka." Her eyes filled with tears. "And Valium. He's killing himself, and I don't know what to do." She turned her face to the wall and pulled a tissue from her purse. "I'm sorry, Jay." She blew her nose, then straightened. "I hated to lay this on you. God knows you've got your own worries." Her eyes flicked out to the dance floor. "If I can watch Todd at home, and you'll be with him at the hotel . . ."

I reached for her hand. "I said I'd keep an eye on him, and I will. But we can do only so much. In the end it's not up to us. If T-bone doesn't care, we can't stop him from crossing the line and screwing up his health."

She nodded, dabbed at her eyes, then gave me a watery smile. I turned toward the dance floor to look at T-bone. The man was obviously feeling no pain.

Neither was Cassy. She danced with her cat's eyes half closed, focused inward, her arms stretched high overhead as she swiveled her hips. Then she captured her thick, shining mane in her hands, combed through it with her long, red-tipped fingers, and released the dark waves with such sexual invitation, my breath caught in my throat.

Suddenly the sharks closed in around her. Had they been there all the time, circling my wife without my noticing them? Or had Cassy sent out signals that had drawn them inexorably to her, smelling her blood as they sliced through the crowd?

I wasn't sure what to do. My instinct was to go out there, but I didn't want to detonate her temper or draw T-bone into a situation that could get ugly, knowing he could waste anyone on the dance floor.

In the midst of my turmoil, I realized Mary was standing beside our table. "I'm going to ask Cassy to go to the ladies room with me."

"Uh, yeah. Good idea."

I watched as she wove through the crowd, took my wife's arm, and said something to her and T-bone. Cassy nodded and followed Mary toward the restrooms. T-bone looked at me with a lopsided grin, shrugged, and kept on dancing. His energy on the floor was the same as his personality, nonstop.

As the calendar approached New Year's Eve, T-bone and I were staggered by the phenomenal sums of money thrown around everywhere for anything. People pressed almost as many five-dollar bills into my palm as one-dollar bills. Vacationers flipped me chips worth five dollars and twenty-five dollars, which weighed down my uniform pockets. If special requests were made, from the best restaurants to the best brothels, many people tipped hundred dollar bills as a thank you.

I found cash on the backseat and floor of many taxicabs, dropped by the previous passengers. Occasionally I found hundreds of dollars at a time. Then the tips became so insanely generous, I couldn't fit all of the night's take in my pockets.

One early morning as I undressed in the locker room, I noticed my thighs were black. How had I bruised myself so badly without realizing it? I wondered, examining myself. Then I realized the rolls of bills had pressed against my quadriceps all night and stained my skin with greasy dirt from the paper money, coins, and chips. It was the color of Vegas money. I tried to wash off the filth, but soap and water hardly made a difference.

The source of all this money was a jam-packed mass of people unlike anything I'd ever witnessed. The noise trapped under the porte cochere became one loud roar. Drunks stumbled into strangers, who shoved them away in disgust. People were yelling, but I couldn't make sense of their words. Most guests looked as if they were having a great time, while others appeared miserable. A few didn't seem to know where they were. The valets, completely overwhelmed by the chaos, ran back and forth in confusion.

I was surrounded by couples, groups, college students, and older people. They wore chinos and an Izod shirt or black tie and tux or went shirtless with a beer gut and sparse, light brown chest hair. Black, white, yellow, brown—people from all over the globe. The whole world had come to Las Vegas to celebrate New Year's Eve.

For a while the cabs couldn't get to the hotel property because the streets were gridlocked. The taxi line snaked around the corner of the building, a good seventy-five yards away. The queue never seemed to move, no matter how hard T-bone and I worked. Sometimes I'd focus on one person standing forty yards from the front of the line and track our progress by when I handed that individual into a cab.

Some of the more observant guests eventually realized they might waste their entire night in a taxi line. They offered us hundred-dollar bills in exchange for a cab or limousine ride on the side.

In the midst of this pandemonium, my buddy Sam materialized at my side, pulled me into a bear hug, and thumped me on the back.

"Oh, man, I owe you big! I got the job with Transportation! Thanks for mentioning me to the coordinator."

"Hey, great!" I disengaged myself. "What're your hours?"

Sam withdrew a sheet of paper from his shirt pocket and held it out to me. "Am I happy about this, especially with the new baby! The timing could not have been better, man. The hotel needed a driver immediately."

I read over his work schedule. He had the graveyard shift.

"Aw, Jesus, Sam, this sucks," I said.

"Nah, this is fine, man," he insisted. "It's what I wanted."

I studied his face, searching for the joke, but he appeared to be perfectly serious. "Okay, man. If you're happy, then I'm happy."

"I ain't happy. I am e-lated. Let me take you out for a drink after your shift, Jay, to thank you."

"You don't have to—"

"Listen up. I *want* to, buddy."

"You mean tonight?" I would definitely need to unwind after the shift. If I weren't dead.

"Yeah. Tonight. I'll be by later."

"Okay. Sure."

He walked off, leaving me to attend to the trio of women at the head of the line. I beckoned to a cab, and a driver I didn't know came roaring up.

"Where are you going, ma'am?" I asked, opening the door.

"Monte Carlo," she answered. "We have dinner reservations there."

"Monte Carlo?" the cabbie exploded. "That place is only three minutes away! You broads could walk there!" He turned on me. "I been waitin' in line for a fare for almost a half hour, and you bring me up for, what, four bucks?"

"Look," I said, feeling bad for him and for the women. One looked a bit frightened. "My job is to help people take a taxi to their destination. *Where* they decide to go is not up to me."

"Maybe *you* don't have a choice where they go," he shouted, "but *I* can decide whether or not to load 'em! Now get me a better fare!"

"And *your* job is to take people anywhere they want to go," I added. When his face flamed red, I tried a philosophical approach. "It all evens out. Sometimes you get distance riders, and sometimes you don't. I'm not asking, I'm telling you to just do it."

His eyes glazed over as he began yelling at the women in the back seat. "Get out!" he ordered.

Two of the women looked stunned. The other, a tiny bird of a matron with orange hair, yelled back. "We are not moving!" She pointed a finger right at his nose. "Now put yourself in gear and take us there!"

The driver jumped out of his vehicle and flung open the back door. When I saw him reach inside to haul one of the women from the backseat, I whistled for Security. The matron, batting at his hands, climbed out with surprising agility and stood to the side.

A crowd gathered, and the cab line was a mess as everyone tried to watch the drama unfold.

Next the cabbie reached in for the feisty redhead.

She reared back, cocking her elbow, and then launched a perfect right jab at his nose. Blood spurted everywhere. I stood gaping as the little woman emerged from the cab and brushed off her skirt and accepted her friends' praise.

"I was assaulted!" the cabbie whined, trying to get my support.

Bug-eyed Dick appeared out of nowhere to lend a hand. Not once did he as my supervisor imply the incident might have been my fault. He kept the onlookers calm, and I was able to return to work.

Security arrived and held the cabbie, who had started to bawl, until the police showed up. As the authorities took him away, the driver cried, "Look at my nose! Look at my nose!"

See a psychologist! See a psychologist! I thought, and went to find the women a taxi. By the time I helped them into a new cab, the red-haired pugilist had become the crowd's favorite and was accepting invitations to meet various people for breakfast the next morning. Their ride drove away, and they turned and waved.

Finally my shift was winding down. I stood alone, left to my thoughts.

"Hi," a soft voice said behind me.

"Hi," I said, and turned to see a very beautiful, very sexy blonde whom I had noticed several times before. When our eyes met, I felt an instant connection flowing between us. I knew right away that she worked the hotel as a hooker, but that didn't prevent her from feeling our chemistry, too. Her blue eyes widened in surprise and her cheeks flushed. "My name is Angel. What's yours?"

"Jay."

She stood facing me, and as we talked about inconsequential things—football, food, and drugs—I felt very relaxed and uninhibited in her company.

"Angel, can I ask you something about what you do? I am truly interested."

Her eyes softly sparkled as they fixed on mine. "Anything you want."

"Do you worry about catching a disease or about some nut getting rough with you?"

Her expression told me I was ignorant. "Not really. I always make sure someone knows where I'm going, what I'm doing, and who I'm with. I always have my cell phone with me. As for the other, we girls are all regulated. We have to get checked out medically each week."

"But you could catch something and not know it."

She flashed me that look again and laughed lightly. "You are too cute. If a guy wants to get laid—which most don't—he has to pay me big bucks. Then I inspect him, wash him, and put the rubber on him."

Her cell phone rang, and she moved a few steps away from me as she answered it and carried on a brief conversation. She came back and hugged me goodbye.

"What if someone gets rough with you?" I asked again, and gestured for a cab.

"Well, shit does happen, you know, like when some cab driver runs over a doorman's foot. You know the risk is there, but you hope it never happens."

I watched Angel's cab merge with traffic on the main drag and wondered why so many of these women fell into this kind of work. Maybe they fled from grapes-of-wrath towns, or farms, or trailers parks where the drudgery was killing them inside. Maybe they had a stepfather or an uncle who left them feeling hopeless about themselves. I stopped myself from trying to figure them out and hoped that we would meet again.

CHAPTER EIGHT

"I started to lose contact with the real world," I told Sam, "but that lasted for only a little while, until I got used to living my life at night. So maybe you'll adjust pretty quick, too."

My friend nodded. "I'll be fine." He seemed preoccupied.

"My skin turned whiter, and sunlight hurt my eyes," I continued.

"You think my skin'll go white?" Without taking his eyes from the road he punched me in the shoulder, then gripped the wheel again. "The amount of traffic still on the roads in the middle of the night just amazes me."

"And that's my only comfort, man—that a lot of people are in the same boat. The roads are jammed, and a thousand markets, restaurants, gyms, carwashes, and other businesses are open to vampire people like me." I thought for a moment. "Although I admit there's something weird about shopping for Wheaties and mouthwash at three in the morning."

"I didn't know vampires use mouthwash. The red kind, right? Nice touch—makes their breath sweet, for the victims."

We relaxed with companionable silence for a few minutes, and I looked out the window, trying to come down off my shift. I realized I had no idea where we were.

"Where the fuck are you taking me for that drink?" I asked. "Des Moines?"

He hesitated a beat. "I found a new place. Thought you might enjoy it. One of the girls there is amazing."

"Sure." Maybe Sam planned to take his hard-on home to his wife."

I found myself pondering his being excited about working the graveyard shift. Why would a happily married man—now a father—be thrilled with such a shitty schedule? It didn't make sense to me. Then I wondered why I felt so suspicious. Call off the dogs, I told myself. Just relax, will you?

"You know, Cassy and I always had the night in common." I said, coming back to the moment. "We prefer the dark—that's the real explanation. We always have. I met her at one in the morning in Santa Monica, where she was tending bar."

I smiled, thinking of those early days. From the beginning Cassy and I always began our date when everyone else was packing it in. We did all sorts of things late at night. One reason we came to Vegas was its being a twenty-four-hour place, a city that breathed at night. We still laughed at how Connecticut had so little nightlife to offer.

I didn't have the hunger for round-the-clock playtime anymore, though. It was great for vacations or when I was younger. Or when my job wasn't so physically and emotionally demanding. Or when Cassy wasn't so demanding. Whatever.

Sam stopped the car, and I looked up at the flashing sign to see where we were: a small topless club off Sahara Avenue, far from the main action of the Strip. "We're here," Sam said, and got out of the car with cheerful eagerness.

"She must be a hell of a dancer, to drive all the way to Des Moines to watch her," I said.

"Yeah, man. She's as good as they get."

"How's your friend Steveland?" I asked, using Stevie Wonder's real name as we walked to the entrance. I was giving Sam the opportunity to admit he had been bullshitting me about their friendship.

"He's good, man. Thanks for asking."

I laughed, indulging him. "So is he working on anything interesting?"

Sam looked at me and hesitated, like trying to figure out where I was heading. "Always, absolutely. But I'm not supposed to talk about it."

"Oh. Hey, I don't want to get you in trouble with your friend," I replied, and held the club door open.

"You do that very well," Sam said as he passed me on the way inside.

I smiled. "Glad you noticed. Some people in management think I'm a natural."

Although we were joking around, I was climbing to the top of my game as a doorman. I was becoming razor sharp with my instincts dealing with people and situations. I was good at spotting potential problems and solved them before they caused trouble. I now knew how to work tips from people, and at the end of each night, was bringing home a good amount of money. Even the other doormen themselves, with the exception of the Weasel, began to respect me. Surprisingly, some of the cabbies wanted to vote for me as "doorman of the year."

A few minutes later Sam and I were inside, settled into stools next to the expansive, shiny black platform where dancers did their thing. All these places looked the same to me, with similar lighting, the usual stools, couches, and stuffed chairs with small round tables. They even smelled the same with a mixture of booze, cigars, cigarettes, and perfume. The music was loud, something Latin. I always liked watching women move to Latin music; it was seductive. A couple of blondes with nonstop legs and improbable breasts writhed on poles in the center of the stage, while a dozen other dancers kept to the perimeter, enticing the oglers into springing for some lap dances.

We ordered drinks and enjoyed watching the entertainment. More accurately, I had fun watching how Sam created traffic backups onstage because the girls were reluctant to pass him by. For a guy who had boxed his way into a championship belt, he was surprisingly good looking, without the usual scars and flat nose most boxers exhibited.

Women loved Sam, and he basked in their adoration. I was learning that my friend had a seductive persona he triggered when ladies were around him. Apparently he had cultivated two smiles, one for his buddies and another for the girls.

I also found the other men's reactions to the girls hilarious—particularly the young guys in Vegas on a college break. They acted like such clowns, I got more enjoyment from watching them than I did staring at the dancers. To me, paying someone twenty bucks to sit on my lap and move around was never a lot of fun, especially since touching wasn't allowed. What was the point? But nothing sold like sex, so these bars were always packed.

I took another sip of my drink and tried again to relax and have fun. Not everything has to have a point, I reminded myself. Jesus. I need another drink.

I turned to check Sam's, flagged the waitress for another round, then directed my attention to the stage.

After a few minutes, I turned to Sam to tell him something, but the words died in my throat. Something odd was going on with him. He looked frozen, not breathing, not blinking. I was afraid he was having a stroke. But then I saw her. Standing above him—us—was the most beautiful woman I had ever seen. She was so spectacular that in a room of beauties who happened also to be naked, no one was looking at anyone but her. I felt embarrassingly like one of those college boys.

"Do you see that, Jay?" my friend said reverently out the side of his mouth. "Oh, shit. Now that woman is all world! She is definitely fine."

"That's Capri," the guy next to us said. "She sort of spoils you for everyone else," he added woefully.

Capri had red-gold hair the color of certain leaves in the fall—the special ones that when you were a kid you stopped to pick them up. The shade had none of the harshness that screamed of chemicals. No, it was thick, it was pure silk, and it was all hers. Her utter perfection extended to her creamy, flawless complexion and eyes too light and golden to be called hazel. Amber eyes, caramel eyes. Honey eyes. Piercing, sexually inviting eyes.

This woman could have stood on the stage, hip cocked, and filed her nails, and it would have grabbed the audience. But she actually moved her body better than the other girls. Men surrounding the stage already had their money out and folded and wedged between their fingers, as they waited hungrily for their turn. Even while another dancer gyrated in their lap, they were watching Capri. I'd never seen anything like it, but as I felt my gaze pulled to her, the situation made total sense.

Capri had to be twenty something, but she appeared younger. Even that was a turn-on as she gyrated like a pro. One sorry bastard who was holding a hundred dollar bill looked about to burst into flames as she hopped off the stage to sit on his lap. She sat between his legs directly on the bulge in his pants and moved in such a way that it hurt me to watch. The guy was stunned and helpless, pressed back against his chair, mouth agape, chest heaving. His nicely cut hair suddenly darkened and flattened to his scalp with sweat, and within minutes his shirt was soaked. Had her performance lasted another thirty seconds, he would have needed to run home and change his pants.

A few times during the routine her searing gaze shot bolts at Sam. I was struck by the shrapnel as he blasted apart beside me. I squirmed with foreboding.

"Jay . . ."

"Yeah, Sam?"

"I have to have her."

Oh, fuck.

Sam and T-bone and just about everyone else I knew had had been unfaithful to their wife, husband, and significant other. I had never broken my commitment to Cassy. It just wasn't in my nature to hurt my wife—or myself—when I already grasped the seriousness of the consequences. But at that moment, Sam was scaring the living shit out of me.

He was hot to possess this stranger's body, this unknown girl who appeared to enjoy the absolute annihilation of the man nearly passed out beneath her. Couldn't Sam see how twisted this was? Lap dances were intended to be harmless fun, making a joke of the torture women's desirability inflict upon men. That's how a lap dance is constructed, with its specific roles and rules: The dancer plays the temptress; the man helplessly endures her teasing. His volcanic sexual tension builds but can't explode in lovemaking—that would break the rules. So instead everyone laughs and smokes and drinks and spends money and buys more dances. They ride the roller coaster again and again.

I saw nothing playful about this red-haired goddess. She broadcast pure, evil power, and I knew for certain that small victories would never satisfy her. She would not only wring a man dry, she'd turn him inside out and fuck him blind.

Sam was a good friend, and I was his. If I didn't do something, he'd be lost. I felt desperate. At that moment, I thought it was a matter of life or death. I wanted to stand up, look him in the eyes, and say, "We're leaving, Sam. Now."

But I didn't, and for the most sorry-ass reason. What blasted into my brain was Bug-eyed Dick, my supervisor, asking me in the employee locker room what I would do if a friend was speeding toward a cliff—Dick's sneaky prelude to saving me from myself through religion. I saw myself about to act like Bug-eyed Dick, like some high-and-mighty shit head thinking he had all the answers for everyone else.

Whatever the reason—maybe it was how much I'd had to drink or how exhausted I was from my shift—in that moment I decided I had no right to interfere in Sam's life. The man was not asking me for help or guidance. Cassy would have been proud of me. She never tossed anyone a life preserver and teased me mercilessly when I became a guidance counselor.

My decision confused me and made me grumpy as hell. I soothed myself by promising to be there for Sam whenever he called me.

The flawless beauty danced forward, and Sam wore his special smile as he opened himself to her. I abandoned my stool to move well out of the way and signaled for another drink while I watched Sam's life come undone.

Capri slid into his lap, and he didn't have a chance. She slowly and deliberately brought her face closer to his, with a look that reflected total sensual focus. She made him believe that he was the one she'd been searching for her whole life. That no one else could make her feel so good. She did it all with her eyes, then her fingers, and finally her body. When she was finished, Sam's eyes had disappeared in his head. He handed her another twenty, then another and another.

"Hey, live and let live." The man from the bar was standing next to me. He motioned with his glass at Sam and snorted in derision.

"The local slogan," I replied.

"The Chamber of Commerce motto."

"Soon to be law."

"Not to mention the Vegas mantra, 'What happens here, stays here,'" he said, then wandered off into the crowd, shaking his head.

Interesting guy, I thought, and felt vindicated that at least one other person besides my wife in this City of Fantasy seemed to agree with my own observations.

When Cassy and I first arrived, she had sensed that Vegas would be a bad place to hold a marriage together, a terrible environment to love somebody. But for us, Vegas was supposed to be a stopover, just dinner at a diner, a place we would stay *over,* not stay *in.*

In the time since we'd been there, I had grown to agree with her. In a twenty-four-hour town where work schedules split into ten different shifts and different days off, relationships literally disintegrated. Month after month, year after year, couples rarely saw each other, let alone spent time together. Of course vows of loyalty and true love went out the window when your, "until death do we part" mate became some stranger who shared your kitchen and garage. When the partnership lost its meaning, Vegas offered countless pleasures, all with impunity.

From its earliest days, Vegas had grown on its reputation for privacy and anonymity. You could be the devil, and no one would notice you. In Vegas, you could pretend to be something you weren't. Tell any kind of story, and no one would doubt you because no one gave a shit if you were telling the truth or not.

The moment visitors stepped off the airplane onto Vegas soil, all the rules changed or, more accurately, disappeared—rules that had grounded those people for a lifetime. For only twenty bucks some poor schmuck could find out what it was like to have a beautiful topless woman with a stunning body sitting on his lap, touching his face and hair, his neck and legs, while her breasts were two inches from his mouth. Or for a few hundred dollars, the Rotarian from Iowa could hire a hooker to fulfill his pubescent fantasies. And if he had a wife and kids, it didn't matter—no one would ever find out.

The fun and games weren't limited to sex and gambling. I had watched as people drank more alcohol, sucked up more cocaine, and squandered more money than they ever would have done at home. Many party animals never slept during their entire stay. That had been their intention from the first. (For that matter, they never ate a meal, changed clothes, or bathed . . . all in the name of blowing off steam.)

When the vacation had ended, when Monday morning rolled around and they had to go back to their desk at work and the family dinner table as the person they used to be, they couldn't. That person no longer existed. There was no going all the way back, no undoing what you'd done.

I believed that once someone crossed a line—any line—that person was changed forever. The brain chemistry was altered. The party animal had permanently set a course down a different road, and no one could predict where the hell it might end or how. That was now a dark secret.

Once these poor sons of bitches realized they had lost their identity, their very soul, in a few days of manic self-destruction, the terror would be too immense to face. Of necessity their defense mechanisms would save them; denial had to transform their horror into a grand illusion that they had had a great time.

Vacationers didn't comprehend that the Strip was as treacherous and almighty an enemy as the ocean. No human could control or understand either one's power. The best anyone could do was battle the current and hope he didn't drift out too far to return to safety. That meant knowing which lines were harmless and which weren't.

Did Sam know the difference? He had at one time, not so very long before, and his integrity was a big deal in our friendship. Now as I watched him arch under the swells of the temptress in his lap, I doubted he'd know his shoe size. Why was he paddling as fast as he could into danger? I could not fully understand it.

I thought about my own marriage. Where was Cassy at that moment? Probably in our bed, asleep. So why wasn't I with her? Suddenly I wanted very much to go home.

I ordered another drink and took a large gulp, feeling very pissed off. The evening was supposed to be a thank-you from Sam for mentioning him to the head of Transportation. Some piss-poor show of gratitude, Sam. Fuck you very much, buddy. When he had invited me out, he knew exactly what he was doing. I felt a little pissed off and sad at the same time.

Eventually he stumbled his way over to me. He looked as if he had been electrocuted.

Good friends that we were, I was waiting for him and helped him out to the car.

"But it's New Year's Eve, Jay!" Cassy yelled. "I can't believe I'm alone on fucking New Year's Eve! Management should have worked out some special schedule at the hotel—you know, like bringing everyone in to work but giving them shorter shifts. At least we could have had a drink together like normal people."

The last thing you need is a fucking drink, I thought angrily, but I managed not to say it. My wife sat ramrod straight in a dining-room chair. Posture was one of the giveaways she'd been drinking too much. I had known her long enough to recognize all the signs of alcohol particular to her. No one else might notice them, but to me, she was a veritable multisensory broadcasting system. Like the mints. As soon as I came through the door from running spec-house errands, her breath had hit me like a blast of Arctic air. For her, the combination was inviolable: vodka and mints. It was sort of comical, if you thought about it. The very trick she used to mask her drinking was exactly what called my attention to it.

"Cassy, management doesn't care if we have a social life. A hotel can't organize around the holiday preferences of its employees."

"Well, it should!" Her gestures served as another signal for me. When she was drunk, she focused on how she used her hands, and her movements became deliberate but delicate. "Managers should always care about keeping the staff happy."

I couldn't help but laugh, her remark was so ridiculous in light of the actual situation. "Management expects us to be happy because of the money we make. The higher-ups already resent us for what we bring in, in tips. And if we don't like it, a thousand guys are in line to take my job."

"All right, *all right!* It's just not fair that I should be alone tonight. Night after night I'm home alone in Las Vegas. It's not like we live in fucking Peoria, Jay! We're in the ultimate party town, and there are a thousand things to do. So what am I doing? Nothing! Shit." She covered her face with her hands and sobbed, her shoulders hunched and shaking.

"Cassy," I said gently, "your sitting at home every night isn't good for either of us."

She looked at me between her fingers. "Is Todd working?"

"What do you mean? He and I are a team. Of course he's working," I answered quickly. "Everyone is."

"What's Mary doing?"

"I'm sure she has to work tonight, too."

"All right, all right . . ." Cassy got up and walked into the kitchen, to where her purse sat on a counter. The department store issued clear plastic satchels to the employees, to discourage pilfering product into their purses or backpacks. She dug out a tissue and blew her nose.

Seeing all her inventory exposed like that was sort of cool, I thought. I tried to make peace. "Your purse reminds me of the Centre Pompidou," I said. "You know, with all the pipes and ductwork exposed?"

"Well, if you like it so goddamned much, Jay, why don't you do it at your beloved spec house?" she asked nastily.

Pow. The more Cassy drank, the more cynical, the nastier, her mouth. I hated being around her. Who wouldn't? Todd and Mary didn't have fun around Cassy when she was out of control. Her attitude was the main reason, T-bone had confided, why he and Mary didn't want to go out anymore as a foursome. All we ever did together was get really fucking high, then go someplace. We loved to get shit-faced; if anyone deserved the temporary escape from reality, we were it, and we didn't want anybody screwing up our good time.

But while Todd, Mary, and I became more relaxed and comical, Cassy grew increasingly uptight and belligerent.

I wanted to say to T-bone, "When she gets like that, I don't like being around her, either, so how 'bout the three of us taking in a movie next week?" Instead I told him not to worry about it, that I understood. Actually I was disappointed and supremely pissed off with Cassy for lousing up the social life she had demanded I provide.

"I am not going to discuss the spec house with you right now," I said. "I have an insane night ahead of me, and I'm already wiped out from last night's chaos. If you want to talk about the house this week, on my day off, we can do that."

"All right. All right, we will," she sniffed. Cassy overused "all right" when she'd been drinking.

"Fine," I said.

"But you know as well as I do, Jay, that it's going to be *another* financial disaster, just like the fucking Connecticut house."

Her using the Connecticut project as a weapon against me was a low blow, and I felt like strangling her. Instead I gathered the stuff I'd need for work. I'd go early, have something to eat in the employee cafeteria, and try to get centered.

"We'll talk next week, Cassy," I said firmly. "When you're like this, I don't want to have anything to do with you."

She started to wail. "I'm so fucking tired of staying home alone! All the goddamn time, I'm trapped in the house with nothing to do."

I turned on her. I was so angry, I could hardly look at her. "I am not responsible for how you waste your time!" I shouted. "Take classes! Volunteer at the hospital—"

"I want to have fun!" she shrieked.

"Then do it, goddammit!" I shouted. "Go have fun! Enjoy your life! If you are so fucking miserable, call up your girlfriends and go out to dinner. Go to a fucking show."

"I will!" she screamed, and jumped up. "Starting tonight!"

"I hope you do, Cassy." I felt strangely calm. Something had slammed shut inside me. I had shut down emotionally and withdrawn from her.

I couldn't stand how argumentative and cynical she had become. I didn't like the look in her eyes or how she smelled. I hated how her sarcasm had cut me again and again and again with its hard, sharp edge. It was steadily severing our bond, shredding our closeness.

As I walked to the car, I weighed the risk of telling Cassy to enjoy herself. No doubt some man would find my wife attractive. He would introduce himself and ask if he could buy her something at the bar. She wouldn't be able to turn down free booze or stop herself at one drink. If she were drunk and frustrated, or if he were persistent and admiring, she might be tempted to cross the line with him.

And how would you feel about that, old boy? I asked myself.

Even though I knew landmines were hidden all over town, I always trusted Cassy. A smooth guy at some bar might entice another man's wife, but not mine. She would never betray me— we had come too far together.

I forced myself to consider it anyway. I had seen it happen to others so many times. I tried to get quiet with my thoughts and float above my anger, so I'd hear the truth, spoken inside my heart.

You and Cassy haven't truly bonded and aren't soul mates, it told me. You stay together for other reasons. You don't want to be alone. Her fears and neuroses are compatible with yours. Truth?

Yes, yes, and yes.

Her going out to the clubs without me would lift the guilt and the pressure from my shoulders. I could stay home and rest my body enough to do my job and not give a shit about whether or not Cassy was bored.

I started my car and backed out of the driveway. I took a long look at the façade before shifting into first gear. I would not be returning to the same place when my night was over. Oh, it would be the same four walls on the same square of sandy dirt, but with Cassy out all night on New Year's Eve, drinking, maybe doing drugs, and looking for the fun and freedom she didn't have with me—well, it just wouldn't be *our home* anymore.

CHAPTER NINE

Even before the blowout with Cassy, I had planned to get to work early on New Year's Eve. I changed into my uniform in the locker room, and as I passed through the adjacent baggage area, I noticed the woman from Human Resources who had interviewed me as an applicant.

She stood in the glassed-in bell-captains' office, which was situated in the center of the cavernous room. Her small chin was tilted up, and her arms were folded across her chest as she read the memo Bug-eyed Dick had taped to one of the walls reserved for announcements. I hadn't focused on its content too closely because the festive red-and-green border, drawn by a child's hand, obviously did not indicate official hotel business. I knew the flyer had to do with religion, included a schedule for church services where Dick was a deacon, and exhorted us all to aspire to new heights of spiritual awareness in His name during the holiday season.

The poster hadn't offended me, but it pissed her off plenty. From twenty feet away, I could see red blotches darken her throat and then travel up into her cheeks as she peeled the sheet of paper from the wall. Then, hands on her hips, she turned a full circle to look at the faux-fir loopy garland taped along the office walls near the ceiling. She paused only briefly while facing the foot-tall fiber-optics tree atop a four-drawer metal file cabinet.

Uh-oh, I thought. Dick would be hearing about this, I knew. His memo and some decorations violated hotel policy. I felt certain his being a supervisor made his violation inexcusable in her eyes.

Dick had not tried to lecture me about religion again, but his attitude toward me had changed completely. No longer was he friendly and laid back. The simplest requests, which at one time he had granted as a matter of course, he now denied without even considering them. His behavior angered and inconvenienced me, but I hoped in time things would settle back into their old rhythm.

Now the woman's gaze focused on a lidded cardboard file box on the desk Dick shared with the other captains. She upended the box, dumping its contents unceremoniously across the neatly organized workspace, then collected the garland, and the church announcement into the box, replaced the lid, and carted it toward the baggage-room door.

I didn't know how deep or wide the ripple effects of Dick's actions would be, but my instincts told me I should make her aware of my presence. I said hello. She nodded at me, and her jaw was set.

"Would you like a cart for—?" I asked her.

"No, thank you." She answered without breaking stride. In an odd way, I felt relieved as I watched her march away. I knew it was stupid, but I suddenly felt it was okay to be a Jew, for now. I turned the other way and headed to the stairs.

Usually as I walked down the long hallway to the underground dining hall that served the hotel's seven thousand employees, the noise met me halfway. With its multiple television monitors blaring, hundreds of workers talking, dishes and silverware clinking, and every sound echoing off the walls, the place creates a racket beyond belief.

Tonight, although the room was packed with bellmen, clerks, waitresses, and dealers, everyone was strangely quiet, subdued. I guessed they must be conserving their energy for the night ahead. Serving the masses would require everything we had to give, and then some.

I took my cue from them and found an isolated table. I sure as hell wasn't in a socializing mood anyway. I ate my sandwich undisturbed, except for the thoughts about my life. I tried not to get moody about what was happening at home with Cassy. I owed T-bone a focused and functioning work partner, especially with his back so fucked up.

The constant demands on Todd's body took their toll on him. He'd began to complain about his neck or his stomach or his back. His back seemed to cause him the most discomfort. Had Mary not mentioned Todd's problems, I wouldn't have paid attention because I was in constant pain, too.

My body begged for rest, but Todd and I couldn't take time off to heal. The Grand was the new kid on the block. The events and shows kept coming, and the money was like a drug. I was beginning to suspect that Todd and I brought in more cash than any of the other doormen at the hotel. Our shift was right in the midst of all the action: the dinner crowds, convention goers, and nightlife ticket holders arriving and departing; the people pouring out during all the show intermissions, the event breaks. For us, taking time off meant a big loss of revenue.

Being a doorman was the best tipping job in the city—depending upon the hotel. Each resort had its own target group. Some looked for families, others aimed for the twenty- and thirty-something singles crowd, still others courted upper-class adults. The guests at Caesar's Palace and at Bellagio were known for generous gratuities, but the people staying at Circus Circus had the reputation of being tightfisted. Some hotels had much more volume than others, so at the end of a shift, the sheer numbers made for a good night. The season, the shift, and the schedule of shows and special events influenced the tips, too. I knew the Grand was about as good as it gets; we had everybody, and we offered everything.

I looked around at my colleagues. Some of them appeared familiar to me, from the training and orientation sessions. During casual conversations, most said they'd consider their job at the hotel as temporary, a stepping-stone. Everyone wanted something else, something more weighty and respectable— a *profession*.

My eyes settled on a trio of men in their fifties hunched over their meal. Their uniform identified them as maintenance engineers. I watched them for a few moments, the easy demeanor achieved by coworkers with many years of association. They'd probably worked together at their previous job. A middle-aged employee anywhere, at any hotel, was not that common. Not so long before, Vegas had been a place where people stayed in their job for thirty to forty years. Keeping their nose clean was enough to earn job security. Now, no one wanted to stay in Vegas for that long.

What about me? I wondered. Cassy and I had already lived there longer than we had planned. With our relationship in flux, I wasn't so sure Vegas would be a stopover for me. The money I brought home was much more than I had guessed. And one thing was certain: On New Year's Eve the money would be phenomenal—a windfall.

That reminded me of D-man and the diamond wedding ring he'd found in a taxi. I'd have to ask T-bone for an update.

Once I reached the porte cochere and saw the harried grin on T-bone's manic face and the massive crowds, I knew the tips exceeded *great* and had reached the realm of *insane*. Money was thrown around everywhere for anything.

"Thanks for comin' early, man," he said. "This is unbelievable."

Between the two of us, we were able to pick up the pace . . . not that it made any difference. The guests just kept coming.

"I'd like to go to the Mirage," a sixty-something accountant-type said as the next taxi stopped in front of us. I opened the door, he got in; I closed the door, the taxi sped off.

I turned to the next in line, a woman looking back toward the lobby. "Ma'am?" I said to get her attention. "Where would you like to go?"

She turned to me, then frantically looked around us.

"Where's my husband?" she shrieked.

"Who—?" I realized her husband was the guy I had just sent to the Mirage. Why hadn't he stopped me from closing the door of the cab? Or tell the driver to stop? Had he forgotten his wife was with him? Unbelievable! I guess he couldn't wait to get on with his time on the strip.

Wearing a tight dress and high heels, she hurried as best she could after the long-gone cab.

That could only happen here, I thought.

As the night wore on, the crowds never diminished. Every once in a while T-bone and I exchanged looks of incredulity. He was as hyper as I've ever seen him. He had to have ADHD. He couldn't focus on anything.

Or maybe he's high, I suddenly thought. His mind is going at the speed of light.

I watched as he opened a cab door for a baldheaded man and at the same time carried on a conversation with a couple in the cab line, behind him. Without looking Todd slammed the cab door and nearly decapitated the bald gentleman.

"Whoops! Sorry, sir. Are you all right?" he asked.

The bald man looked a bit wobbly, but T-bone, not missing a beat, turned back to the couple. "As I was saying," he continued, "you want to catch 'O' at Bellagio. That's still the best show in town for my money."

My body ached. Todd and I would have to relax, or we'd never be able to handle Sunday, when the masses would head for home, all at the same time. I fielded so many questions, filled so many special requests, helped so many people . . . I felt detached from reality, in a dream state. Am I in *The Twilight Zone*? I took some deep breaths to bring myself back to where I needed to be, and then I whistled for the next taxi in line.

Oh, shit. The Candy Lady. I could see her bouncing up and down in her seat. I knew what I had to do. I blew the whistle, then crouched down like a catcher at the ready behind home plate.

The window to her right was open, as usual, and I could hear her scream, "Here! Take it! Take it!"

A piece of candy sailed out the cab window in my direction. I never knew if the goodies she kept in a bag beside her would be chewy or hard, wrapped or unwrapped. All I knew was that I had no choice but to snatch the missile from midair; otherwise it would whack one of the guests behind me. Once, I called out, "No! Don't! I don't want—!" She winged it anyway. Tonight, perhaps because of New Year's Eve, the Candy Lady hurled a bag of Skittles at me.

"Thanks," I called out, resigned. "And Happy New Year!"

"Yeah! Youse, too." She bounced in her seat as the passengers settled in, and she was still bouncing as she drove away, probably from all the sugar in her body.

I looked around, not knowing what to do with the bag of candy in my hand. I didn't have anyplace to put it, and I couldn't leave my station to toss it. I whistled for another cab, deciding I'd give it to the driver and wish him a good new year.

As luck would have it, Pigpen pulled up. Some cabbies wore a white shirt and a conservative necktie and carried a little can of air freshener mounted on their dashboard. As they drove up to me, they would activate the aerosol, and I could actually see the cloud of mist filling the interior. When I opened the door, a distinct fragrance—pine, cherry, or citrus—would clear my sinuses.

When I opened Pigpen's door, however, a specific odor would assail me. Sometimes it was french fries, sometimes onion rings, sometimes cigarette smoke, sometimes *him*. The condition of the interior of Pigpen's cab was as bad as its smell. Soda cans, papers, crumpled fast-food bags, and other garbage littered the seats, the dashboard, and the floor. The windows were foggy.

I had always wanted to talk to Pigpen, an impulse left over from my days studying Abnormal Psychology, but he never said a word. In fact, he never reacted in any way. He didn't seem to care if his fare wanted to go across the street or a hundred miles away. He just stared straight ahead and did the job. I wondered if he ever had a lobotomy.

I got his passengers settled into the back, then held out the Skittles. "I'd like to give these to you, man."

No reaction.

"You're, uh, good to work with."

Silence.

"So have a good new year."

Nothing. I set the bag gently on the seat and closed the door.

As he drove away, he gently tapped the horn. Twice. A miracle.

I glanced at my watch. Four-thirty. I was hungry and thirsty and felt beaten up. The pockets of my pants were pressing against my thighs, bulging from the money I had made. I had earned every penny. The job was physically grueling, not just from spinning around while opening doors for people but from keeping everything under control.

I stared at the spectacle playing out all around me. Knowing that the air was moving helped me feel better, calmer, so I lifted my gaze above the churning crowd and focused on the palm trees to my left. I saw a breeze moving the fronds. The porte cochere seemed less claustrophobic to me, and the crush of people less malevolent.

The porte cochere area was quieter now. I looked at my watch. Five-fifteen. The sun would be rising soon. I looked around for Todd and found him standing under the palm trees, looking as tired and spent as I've ever seen him. He and I had worked well beyond the end of our shift.

I walked over to him. He was rubbing his lower back and grimacing. "You okay?"

He shook his head in disgust. "Fucking back. Shit."

"If it's just your back that hurts, you're doing good. I hurt all over. This was insane. But we made great money."

"Yeah," he said, almost begrudgingly. Then, "Jay, I've got an idea for a business we can do on the side, make a little extra money, sock it away—something to add to our tips."

"I'm listening."

T-bone knew some guy who knew some other guy who worked at the only all-Spanish radio station in Vegas, and *he* had a cousin who worked at a cigar factory in Cuba.

"He can get us anything we want," T-bone said.

"Jesus." I whistled low. The country was right in the middle of a cigar craze. "There's a huge market for Cuban smokes just because they're so fucking hard to get."

"So you in?"

"I'm in."

"Should we start with, what? Ten boxes?"

"Let's try twenty. I think they'll go fast."

"Done."

"Thanks, man." The offer helped me feel better about T-bone. Including me in the deal sort of balanced out his not wanting to put up with my wife's bullshit anymore.

I trudged back to my station as a couple of people stumbled out of a cab. They looked hung over and exhausted. Other tourists mulled around aimlessly, seeming not to have a destination. I wasn't sure why, but I began to feel intensely angry.

I wanted to yell, "Hey! Zombies! You couldn't be done yet! This is Las Vegas! There's a thousand, maybe two thousand restaurants that serve breakfast. You'd have to stay here eighteen years to try 'em all, but don't let that notion overwhelm you. Come on people get started! You want a French breakfast? Italian? Japanese? It's *your* choice, assholes."

My speeding thoughts were in a jumble, more hostile than funny. It was time for me to go home and pass out.

CHAPTER TEN

"Good evening." I said to the next person in the cab line—a big, robust man with rosy cheeks. "How can I help you?"

"Caca Sherom," he said in a thick accent as he lit a foul-smelling cigarette.

"Excuse me?"

"Otel Caca Sherom."

"I'm sorry, sir. I don't understand," I said, beckoning a cab.

The taxi pulled up, and the man got halfway in so I could not close the door. Puffing madly on his cigarette, he pointed at the cabdriver and ordered me in an angry voice, "You tell!"

"What?" I asked. *Aw, shit, here we go.* My anxiety level shot up.

"You tell drri-ver Caca Sherom Otel. Say otel!"

The cabbie contorted to look out at me through his window. "Where's he wanna go?"

I stood unmoving as the big man screamed at me in a foreign language sprinkled with almost-English. "Somma bo bitchy to you! I tell you up to here! Everybody say to you!"

The cabbie stared at me, incredulous, as the man settled in his seat and slammed the car door shut. As the vehicle pulled away, the bastard flicked his cigarette, hitting me on the chest.

I had noticed from day one on the job that a lot of vacationers were edgy, hostile, or enraged. They were nasty to each other and vicious to the Grand's staff. What was going on? Why weren't they relaxing and enjoying their visit?

Finally I had enough experience to figure out the cause: The most antagonistic guests by far were the gamblers. They sat in the casino hour after hour without eating, sleeping, drinking enough to stay hydrated, or moving around. They rode the currents of adrenaline, up, down, and losing track of time and their money as the casino's electrical charge quickened their heart rate, raised their intensity, and infused them with power. Once they were vibrating with high energy, Lady Luckless, the devil-goddess of the Vegas Empire, pulled the plug on the car payment, tuition, child support, and maybe next month's mortgage.

The losers stumbled outside to the porte cochere, and just as the self-loathing began to penetrate their consciousness, there I stood. I had resigned myself that being a whipping boy was as much a part of my job as recommending good restaurants.

Now, I picked up the smoldering cigarette butt and tossed it in the trash, and as I brushed ashes off my uniform, I looked around for Sharkey or Bug-eyed Dick or some other supervisor. I was grateful no one from management had witnessed that guy's bullshit; more than enough dislike already ricocheted between the doormen and our bell captains. Sharkey and the other supervisors had begun harassing us during our training classes, and their threats of dismissal had never stopped.

The captains thought we doormen needed to learn humility. According to them, we were an elite group making too much money. Yes, we did well financially, but we worked our asses off for our tips. The captains didn't seem to give a shit about that.

So T-bone and Weasel complained about Sharkey to top executives, and within days, the hotel had become a war zone. The negative energy of a battlefield swirled around the porte cochere, and I was turning into a basket case.

Sharkey had been dangerous before T-bone and Weasel complained to management; now he was lethal. He still believed I had ratted on him, even though I professed my innocence.

I tried to stay clear of him, but that was impossible. His character had no room for compromise and whenever he looked my way, his eyes were more piercing than ever. He wrote notes after our every interaction, documenting what had been said, then filed them in my permanent folder in the Human Resources office.

My anxiety intensified in direct proportion to my supervisor's rising anger. I knew if I didn't do something to defuse the situation, my own rage would be uncontrollable. If I blew, I'd be out on my ass.

The only way to wipe my blood off Sharkey's teeth would be for T-bone and Weasel to fess up. I didn't expect much from Weasel, but Todd and I were friends and partners. He had always assured me that if I ever needed him, he would be there for me. I decided to tell him the time was now to come through for me, and tell Sharkey the truth.

That settled, I returned my full attention to my job just as a debonair man emerged from the lobby. This was a good omen, I decided.

"Hello," I said. "Where are you headed?"

"I'd like to go to hell or the morgue," he replied.

That stopped me. "Uh, trouble in the casino?" I asked as I gestured for a cab.

"Well, let's put it this way," he answered. "I'd like a cabdriver who will help me kill myself by crashing the car."

When I saw whose cab stopped beside us, I knew the man's losing streak still had steam. I tucked the guy into the backseat of Pigpen's cab and, shaking my head, watched them speed away.

The definition for *suicide*: not coping, Las Vegas style. I hated hearing about it. The most common acts were people leaping off their hotel balcony or putting a bullet in their skull and letting housekeeping find them.

All night long, sirens wailed up and down the Strip, and whenever their urgent wail came close, I shuddered, wondering if the emergency was at the Grand.

If an ambulance pulled up under our porte cochere, the happy vacationers in the cab line stopped talking just long enough to watch the paramedics run inside with their gurney. People whispered that someone in the casino must have committed suicide.

If we were lucky, the EMTs would wheel out a guest who was merely having trouble breathing. I returned to my work, relieved to know the patient would be okay. I myself experienced difficulty breathing every night. Stress.

Weird: in the beginning, I enjoyed the excitement, the pace, the performance. Todd and I had fun and joked around with the valets and cabbies. I had lost my center on New Year's Eve, and now, after so much time had passed, I still couldn't get my bearings, at work or at home. I felt disoriented, trapped in a demented funhouse where the floor fell away and nothing was secured.

I expected the grueling, punishing job to wear me down eventually. I just hadn't expected it to happen so quickly.

This was not life, I realized with a jolt; it was surrealistic theater in the round. I was not a player in on the joke; I was a stunned observer coming unglued, courtesy of the MGM

Grand's special-events calendar. Each celebration was extreme, bizarre, and absorbing. Every target group brought its own culture to Las Vegas, with a unique language, specific customs, and rules for acceptable behavior.

In January we hosted full-blown Chinese New Year festivities. The swell of Chinese tourists was astonishing. The city's traditional dragon parade surely put San Francisco's to shame. Casinos offered special chips to commemorate the Year of the Ram, and the Grand served special menus, booked Chinese entertainers, and redecorated the lobby in red and gold to represent happiness and wealth. The brilliant marketing efforts paid off: the fifteen-day holiday became the second largest in gaming revenues.

Suddenly the dried bean curd, black moss seaweed, and ginkgo nuts disappeared from the restaurants, replaced by mountains of barbequed chicken and ribs, barrels of cornbread, and vats of coleslaw and molasses baked beans. The rodeo finals were in town. Trucks brought in enough beer to flood the Red River Valley. Within forty-eight hours, thousands of quarter-sized splats of spent chewing tobacco stained every square foot of my work area.

Wham! Trade in the cowhands' extravagant sideburns for the Orthodox Jewish men's *peyos,* said to deemphasize the importance of appearance. Gone were the wranglers and ten-gallon hats. Instead the cab line was a bobbing sea of rounded, black-felt chapeaus. The Hasidim were in town for the International Jewelers' Convention.

My head was spinning. No surprise, then, that I began to suffer from tics, compulsions, and unconscious, self-soothing behaviors. I vigorously rubbed my thumb against the knuckle of my forefinger while blinking my eyes more than usual. I continually checked for a breeze in the palm fronds. Periodically I would open my mouth as far as my lips would allow. At the same time, I habitually checked to make sure my zipper was up, my shoes were shiny, and my tie was straight. I must have looked like an obsessive-compulsive cartoon character. When I noticed what I was doing, I got pissed off at myself. Things had to change. Maybe deep breaths. Maybe getting drunk.

I walked over to where Todd stood.

"What's up, my brother?" was the first thing out of his mouth.

"Todd, things have been bad between Sharkey and me."

"Fuck that piece of shit, Jay. Ignore his fuckin' ass." T-bone was already foaming at the mouth.

"I can't. He's on the warpath, and it's wearing me down. I come here every single day worried I'll be told to clean out my locker. I feel I'm being watched constantly, no matter where I am. It really sucks."

"Ya know what, man? You need to keep your ass clean. Just do the job. Sharkey ain't going to fire you. He can't! He needs a reason, and he ain't got jack. So just keep quiet, show up, work, and leave."

I stared at him for a few seconds and knew I needed to get through to him. "How about we take our dinner break together tomorrow?" I asked. "I want to talk about this some more."

"On Sunday?" he asked, surprised. "It can't wait until—"

"I'd really like to get this handled."

"Okay, then. Sure."

I began to feel good that this whole thing might finally come to an end.

Sunday was, without question, the most physically demanding day at work. The length of the taxi line often exceeded a hundred yards, and Todd and I worked quickly for hours, one of us loading the departing vacationers' luggage into the taxi's trunk while the other helped the people settle into the backseat.

Suitcases were always heavy—the average was forty pounds—and most people brought two bags each. Many guests required special assistance. That Sunday T-bone and I lifted a quadriplegic into the front seat of a cab, then we had to heft his three-hundred-pound, battery-powered wheelchair into the trunk. While all this was going on, people were asking us a hundred questions, from wanting a seafood restaurant to finding a gay bar.

After a couple hours of this, my strength and energy were depleted, and each item felt much heavier than it actually was. My muscles always burned like fire on Sundays and ached like hell on Mondays.

The remainder of the week was no picnic, either. The Grand had its own convention center, theme park, and showrooms. When a convention or some big event such as a concert or boxing match drew capacity crowds, everyone usually wanted to go home at the same time.

Since the Grand had opened, though, my partner and I had done a good job. We challenged ourselves to work harder than anyone else. Committed to keeping ourselves in top form to handle the brutal demands of our job, he and I faithfully went to the gym to lift weights. For the most part the strategy worked, but I could see Todd's back pain had worsened since New Year's Eve.

Yet no other doormen in the city could do what he and I did together. We had developed a system, gotten used to operating as a team, and become known as "the workhorses." We'd go full tilt without a break, and when coworkers brought us sodas or sandwiches, the food was likely to sit untouched at the desk.

We supported each other in other ways, as well. Sometimes the guests who were drunk or high on drugs became abusive or insulting. Being treated like shit tore me apart, more than it did the other doormen. Did my being much older than most of my coworkers make me less resilient? Or was respect more important to me than to them because of my personality type? Whatever, T-bone would grab my shoulders, stare into my eyes, and say, "They're under the influence. The drug is talking, man. Don't take it personal."

Whenever we were slammed, we'd contact various taxi companies and tell them to send all available cabs immediately. As soon as the taxis roared up, we would *double load*—fill two vehicles at a time with passengers and luggage.

Often Todd and I drew an audience. People came with their video camera to tape us in action. We had laughed and spun and kicked and danced to call up cabs, to the delight of the guests.

Before the mess with Sharkey and Bug-eyed Dick, management sometimes watched us labor at triple speed. Seconds counted. When the dust cleared, the suits would shake our hand and tell us we were amazing. To them, a fast cab line meant good customer service. To us, it meant more and higher tips.

With a work partner that strong, a bond that close, I had half expected Todd to fess up to Sharkey without any prompting from me. It's what I would have done. Whenever one of my friends was in trouble, loyalty usually took me to one of three places: I could jump in without much forethought and let the fists fly; I could think about the situation before jumping in with both feet; or I could wait until things cooled, then take action. Although in retrospect the last option made the most sense, that had rarely been my style.

As our dinner break approached, I made plans to tell T-bone exactly what I needed him to do and why. I wasn't going to be soft with him. He had been raised on the streets and should instinctively know what the code of friendship demanded of an honorable man—not just for me but for everyone who'd been brought down.

T-bone's and Weasel's little stunt had caused a shitload of problems; no doorman trusted anyone else on the team, and for good reason: we would have gladly sacrificed a coworker to the deep waters to keep our job. After Todd had taken responsibility for his actions, maybe the damage could be undone among our group. And maybe the captains and doormen would call a truce. Maybe Sharkey would get off my back. Maybe I could finally calm the fuck down.

Maybe Dick would eventually chill out. Wasn't he all about love and forgiveness? Maybe, in time, he would have an epiphany that his proselytizing had no place at the Grand, and then he and I would find our way back to something better than we had now.

Maybe.

I knew I was obsessing, but of all the Grand's doormen, I was the only one already in deep shit with *two* direct supervisors. As the human equivalent of a flashing neon bull's-eye, I had concentrated for weeks on staying out of trouble. I kept my mouth shut. I never complained to anyone or suggested better ways to handle a problem—a time-tested method everyone else used to suck up to management. I tried to fade into the woodwork, but invisibility proved impossible because Bug-eyed Dick and Sharkey wanted my ass.

Next I tried to practice the fine art of hotel politics. The more management people liked me, the better my odds of staying employed. Putting it into practice was an exhausting task. I couldn't even figure out where to start ingratiating myself. I had eight immediate supervisors, each with his own rules and interpretations of those rules, his own set of boundaries, and his own personality. One captain was nice, another, a monster. One guy had to be in control; another was too confused to make a decision.

Above my immediate eight supervisors stood a management team more populous than the employee roster. A round-the-clock operation required three shifts of management, and every department—there were a lot of departments—had a handful of supervisors. Each person was responsible for a specific area of the department, but the entire hotel seemed to be a gray area of who was in charge of whom. There were presidents, vice-presidents, assistant vice-presidents, directors, managers, assistant managers, supervisors, captains, leads, and a slew of titles that seemed invented on a whim, solely for the Grand.

I assumed some sort of internal hierarchy lent order to the system, but I sure as hell couldn't figure out what it was—and until I made sense of it, hotel politics would be no help at all.

That night Todd and I walked together to the cafeteria, got our food, and found an isolated place to sit and talk. He set his chair back from the table, stretched out his long legs in front of him, and gestured to me to begin.

I took a deep breath. I had zero appetite. "Todd, I can't keep taking this shit for you and Weasel. I need you to do the right thing."

He stared back at me like I was nuts. "You know what, man? What's important is that management carved Sharkey a new asshole. *Who* reported him isn't important."

"It's important to me, Todd."

"Weasel and I don't need to get credit for telling the suits to get their shit straight." He forced a laugh, but the fear was obvious in his eyes. I studied his face, trying to understand what could possibly be going on in his brain. The issue seemed so black and white to me.

"I can't believe you're turning me down." I was so angry, my voice was shaking. "We're talking integrity here, man, and honor. Not to mention friendship based on mutual trust. I thought all that shit was important to the marines. Did you forget about personal ethics as soon as you left the corps?"

His face flamed deep red, and he looked down at his food tray.

"I brought my loyalty to our friendship," I continued, "and I expected the same from you. Instead I'm here twisting in the wind, and you're saying that's not important."

He met my gaze, and he seemed destroyed. "That's not how it is for me," he said quietly.

"Then why don't you explain it to me," I said coldly.

"You've got to look at the big picture." He pushed his tray aside and leaned forward on his elbows. "This job is all I've got, Jay. I'll never be more than what I am right now."

"But—"

"I'm a beast of burden, man—a fucking mule. When my back goes, I'm done for. You? You've got a degree. If something happens, you can move on, get another job somewhere. I can't."

I struggled to stay in my chair. I wanted to slap him. "What are you saying? That you're not going to do anything? We both know that in a day or a month, some drunk'll lose big at a table and decide to take it out on me. And if he's mad enough and spread around enough money, I'll be fired—because of you, Todd. Because of the strikes I've got against me because of some-thing *you* did! You know that, don't you?"

"I'm truly sorry, man, but I can't help you. If some scumbag jumped your ass, I'd be right there for you. But this is different. Besides, no way is that asshole going to fire you."

T-bone hitched his chair up to the table and tucked into a mound of mashed potatoes. "You need to calm down, Jay. Take a few days off. Go somewhere with Cassy and rest up. Out of sight, out of mind. This whole fucking thing'll blow over soon." He glanced at his watch. "Shit! It's late! We gotta get back to the line." He shoveled a couple more forkfuls of potatoes into his mouth and stood up.

I got up, too, feeling unsteady. The fuck had actually said no. I was shocked and furious, unable to speak. We walked quickly back toward our workstation without exchanging another word. We were halfway down the long corridor when my cell phone rang. Todd stopped as I pulled the phone out of my pocket. I didn't recognize the number on the display. "You go ahead," I told him. "I'll be there in a minute." Into the mobile I say, "This is Jay."

"Jay! Rocco!"

Rocco was an old acquaintance who supplied the hotels and restaurants with their alcohol. Because of his position, he knew a lot of people. "Hey, man, good to hear your voice! What's up?"

Pause. "This is awkward for me, Jay, but I'm at a club with Cassy—"

"What?"

"Not *with* your wife"—he cleared his throat—"but in the same club. She's all over the place, Jay, and I didn't feel right just, you know, just letting it go. She's drunk, this fuckin' scumbag bartender keeps pouring her drinks. She's talking to everyone . . ." He trailed off. "I'm sorry."

"No, man," I said from the bottom of the well. "You did the right thing. Really."

"Slow dancing."

"What?"

"With men who look like they're from out of town. Dancing, you know, slow. Jesus, I'm sorry to . . ."

I didn't remember ending the call. When I came back to myself, I was under the porte cochere, working the cab line. T-bone had gone home, and I had two more hours before my shift ended. I spent them thinking of my wife in some nightclub, dancing to a ballad, encircled by a strange man's arms, his breath on her neck, her breasts pressed against him.

And I couldn't do a fucking thing about it. I was trapped at the head of a line of drunks, and I was dressed like a clown on a safari. I felt pale, weak, as if my lifeblood and sanity were pooling on the pavement beneath my feet.

CHAPTER ELEVEN

"Honey, this town is filled with bad endings. Before you realize what's happening, you could find yourself in trouble."

"Oh, Jay, for chrissakes! I'm just entertaining myself while you're at work. You *told* me to go out."

I didn't have high expectations for my talk with Cassy. Rocco had been the first to mention her drunkenness to me, but she was probably smashed every night. No conversation could change that.

"I know, Cas." I felt a sense of dread. Our relationship was on the edge of something not good.

We were at the spec house, screwing antiqued bronze knobs and pulls into the kitchen cabinets and drawers. The interior was coming together while my marriage and the housing market were going south. I'd been doing a lot of the work myself now that Sam was spending every free minute with Capri. Probably his wife thought he was with me.

"I know how to keep guys away from me." Cassy flashed a quick grin. "Remember the dawgs?"

A moment of expansive recollection overcame me. Cassy had been mixing drinks in a swirl of cigarette smoke when I first laid eyes on her in a Santa Monica, California, bar. Her extraordinary beauty made me a regular there, with ten buddies—wild men called "the dawgs." Some of us worked construction, the others were Hollywood stuntmen, and we all knew how to party loud and hard. We knocked back gallons of booze, laughed till we were sick, tried to hit on Cassy, and then did it all again the next weekend. God, it was fun. I had to admit, she kept me at bay for so long, I gave up any hope of scoring with her.

Then one night I came into the club early, without the others, and ordered dinner while I sat at the bar. Cassy waited on me, and we talked for the first time. I thought she was nice. Hoping she had learned from our brief conversation that I wasn't as big an asshole as she'd thought, I asked her out.

"I don't date customers," she'd said with absolute finality, and I didn't challenge her. But I could tell she was interested, and the chemistry between us was powerful.

A few weeks later my sister tagged along to the bar with me and the dawgs. She took one look at Cassy and asked, "Who is that girl? She is gorgeous! Look at her beautiful eyes!"

I filled her in.

Later that night my sister faked a visit to the restroom but actually followed Cassy into a storage area. She introduced herself and then said, "My brother really likes you. I can vouch for his being a good guy. Maybe you could break the rules once and go out with him?"

When I found out what she had done, I wanted to kill my sister, but her lobbying knocked down Cassy's defenses. A week later, when she served the dawgs a tray of tequila shots, my glass had a piece of paper wrapped around the rim. I opened it discreetly and found her phone number written in a neat, feminine hand.

Now I looked at my wife gathering the little plastic bags the knobs had been packed in. She and I had been together for so long. We had shared so much. More than anything I wanted to trust her. I needed her—*us*—to be okay.

I went and put my arms around her and pulled her close. "Yeah, I remember the dawgs," I whispered, my lips brushing her ear. "But what if some guy out there has a sister who ambushes you in a storeroom? Will you go out with him?"

Her reaction surprised me. She pushed me away. "I've had enough of this conversation. You don't have to worry about me. And I really don't appreciate your friends spying on me, Jay." She stopped, and her face flushed. "Are you behind this? Did you ask people to follow me? Because if—"

"Jesus, Cassy! I wouldn't do that! Vegas can be a small town and we know a lot of people."

"All right. All right!" She shot me a warning look, then went back to her task. Her quick, precise movements as she snatched up the last of the plastic wrappers told me she was furious. But when wasn't she, these days?

What was I supposed to do? Lay out for her all the reports I'd gotten from my reluctant but well-meaning friends? Was I supposed to accuse her of lying? Of being in denial? I wanted to but didn't. I tried to make peace.

"I'm not worried about you, Cass. I'm concerned about the guys at the clubs. They don't always listen when a woman says no, and some mistake a slow dance for an invitation to have much more. With the nonstop partying going on here, it's the place where people are more likely to get hurt than anywhere else."

She ignored me.

"It's not like L.A. here, Cassy. People don't have the same controls. Vegas is much more aggressive and raw than Los Angeles. The tourists are less accountable here. If you're out alone at night, you're making yourself vulnerable to crazy people."

"Crazy people are all around us, all the time." She threw the tiny plastic bags at the knobs' shipping box, but they were so small and weightless, they floated back at her. "Or maybe the Grand is the only place in the universe where there aren't any."

"But you could innocently start a conversation with someone who's in town for only a few days—"

"Why don't you lock me up, Jay, so a crazy person can't come within a few blocks of me? Husbands have done that for thousands of years. Would you be able to relax then?"

"—and you won't see him again, and weeks go by."

"This is about *you* not feeling safe, not me."

"But let's say he comes back into town and recognizes you. Maybe he's a nice guy, and he buys you a drink, and you make small talk."

She stopped and looked at me, her green eyes dark with rage. "This is not my issue, Jay. It's about abandonment—your fear of losing people. Because your dad left you, you're afraid everyone is going to leave. Don't you dare lay your shit on me. Find yourself a good therapist and work it out!"

I stepped back, stung, as if she had struck me. Was she right? Was that what this was about? I thought my father loved me, but when I was three years old he left my mother and me. He moved to Vegas and never came back. His disappearance had left a gaping hole in my heart—a psychological wound that I was still dealing with. I was in contact with him now, but the feeling of emptiness and isolation was always there, especially toward the end of my shift. When I was under that porte cochere all alone with the drunks and assholes, I felt no comfort, no connection with anyone. It was not a good feeling.

No! Cassy couldn't dump the whole thing on me. Too many friends had called me, describing her outrageous behavior.

I felt frantic as I looked at my wife. Good judgment told me to shut the fuck up, but I couldn't. She was lying and out of control. I had to stop her, had to make her understand, before she crossed all the lines. Maybe she had already. I reminded her of *Fatal Attraction,* when Michael Douglas hooked up for a quickie with a homicidal maniac. I was sounding irrational, and I knew it.

"I know what I'm doing!" she shrieked, and took to the stairs. She stopped halfway up, clutched the banister, and screamed down at me, "I know what I have to do to be happy. Now stop breathing down my neck and do something about your own fucking life!"

Now that T-bone had made his position clear, my last line of defense for keeping my job was maintaining a good relationship with the visitors. Many were infamous for getting hotel staff fired. One complaint from the convention planners, shareholders, family members of management, coworkers, and the guests themselves was enough for possible dismissal. I never knew who was a high roller, a nut case, or a spotter hired by the hotel, so I was cordial to everyone, even as the tourists constantly reminded us of our subservience and vulnerability.

Whatever ridiculous remark they made, I agreed with them. I laughed at their sorry attempts at humor. I recognized their denial and defense mechanisms and was careful to leave them intact. *Be nice. Be nice, be nice, be nice* became my mantra on the drive to work and throughout the night. Do unto me because I can't do it back to you.

With the cracks in my psychological armor widening and my support system crumbling, I didn't know how much longer

I could stand being fed up, undermined, and demeaned. I had never been one to take much shit from anybody. How many times would I force myself to utter, "Yes, sir" and "Yes, ma'am," hour after hour after hour, all night long? Being nice was becoming less a priority than just keeping myself together.

Valentine's Day weekend, I came unglued. What put me over the edge was knowing my marriage was in a pile of shit and having to spend three days surrounded by ecstatic newlyweds. Throughout the city, chapels offered "theme weddings" and, catering to whatever nuptial fantasy the lovers desired, enjoyed their busiest day of the year. City Hall kept its doors open till midnight, to handle all the marriage-license applicants.

Wherever I looked were brides and grooms dressed formally, casually, and every fashion variation in between: *Star Wars*, Elvis, and clown costumes; matching football uniforms, scuba gear, and wetsuits; Western attire, medieval armor, and even two cardboard boxes—one decorated to look like an ATM machine. The only common thread among the threads was the bride's veil.

Limousine drivers worked twelve-hour shifts through Valentine's Day weekend. Sam had disappeared from my life except for an occasional glimpse of his limo when he had a fare at the Grand, and I hoped to bump into him and be able to sneak a few minutes' conversation.

I finally did see his stretch pull up, but we weren't able to say more than hello. I was shocked by the change in his appearance. Had Capri been vacuuming the blood from his veins and the gray matter from his skull? Only a few weeks before, he had been a serious athlete in training, totally focused on his strength, stamina, and speed. Now his eyes evidenced utter dissolution . . . and mirrored how bad off I was, too.

After he drove off, I helped another bride from a taxi. She wore only a bra and panties with her wedding veil; her groom sported a pair of boxer shorts with boots and a cowboy hat. A few bystanders laughed and applauded in appreciation, and the couple acknowledged the accolades by embracing and kissing. The groom tossed his ten-gallon hat into the air and it spiraled to the pavement. Finally: something that matched my mood.

I felt depressed. I'd known my advice to Cassy came with a risk, and I took that risk because of what was at stake. But my approach had been completely wrong, and I felt like a moron. How could I have misjudged her so badly? I felt some responsibility for the undoing of our marriage.

At a tap on my shoulder, I turned to see a clean-cut young kid standing before a group of five raw-boned guys, also in their twenties, who struck me as farmhands. They all looked alike—same buzz haircuts, same denim clothes, same acne. One distinguished himself by appearing particularly tormented. He was pale, shaky. The others were propping him up. He had to be the groom.

"I'll bet you're here for a wedding," I said.

"Yes sir. Ronald here is gettin' hitched tomorrow, and we want to, uh, do somethin' fer him. Me and my buddies was thinkin' of takin' him to one of them topless places." The spokesman's face flamed bright red.

The members of the pack surrounded me so they could all hear what I had to say. The wide, awestruck eyes and slack jaw were familiar to me already. This was a significant moment for these guys, one they'd never forget. I wanted to make the most of it for them.

"Well, what are you guys looking for?" I asked ingenuously.

They giggled nervously and shoved at one another.

"I mean do you want half-nude or all-nude? You want something raunchy and rowdy? Or maybe something a little classier?"

They looked to their leader. "Well," he said to me, "that's just where we thought you might help us out. We've never been to one of those places. What would you suggest?"

I glanced at the hapless groom. His skin looked grayish white under the artificial lights of the porte cochere.

"We'd like to go to a place where the girls are really nice," the leader added. "Know what I mean?"

I was working hard not to laugh at the boys' squirming. "Do you mean 'nice' as in *friendly* or as in *nice looking*?"

The spokesman leaned forward confidentially and beckoned me to approach. I clearly saw the pimples on his face and wondered if he were old enough to walk through a casino, let alone a topless club.

"We want to fix him up, you know? Get him a girl?"

I stepped back to look at the entire group. "Let me make sure I have this right. You want to get your buddy boozed up and laid by a nice lady, and then you plan to send him off to the showers, stuff him into a tuxedo, and—" I paused for emphasis "—deliver him to the woman he wants to spend the rest of his life with? Right?"

Ronald looked as if he might throw up.

"And I suppose if your fiancée—"

"Britny." He burped.

"Thank you. *Britny* were to find out about this, how you spent your last night as a single man, she wouldn't get upset?"

"You kiddin'?" Ronald said. "She'd freakin' kill me first, then she'd skin these guys alive!"

The group fell silent. Finally Ronald managed to say to his friends, "Hey, y'all, maybe we can just go somewhere to have a couple drinks and hang out for a little while." He turned to me. "You got bowling here?"

"We have everything. This is Vegas, man." I grabbed a cab and stuffed them in. "Hey, Ronald, I hope you and Britny have a good life," I told him, then directed the driver to the resort voted every year to have the best bowling alleys.

I watched them leave. Ronald turned around, and through the back window of the taxi, he gave me a thumbs up.

Suddenly a cab roared up and, tires smoking, screeched to an abrupt stop in front of me. When the driver slammed on his brakes, all four passengers rocked forward in unison and screamed. Oh, Jesus. Cowboy had to be behind the wheel. I peered through the windshield as Security came rushing over, and sure enough, I saw the outline of his ten-gallon hat.

I hurried to open the doors, and four women, all seniors, staggered out of the taxi. No one spoke.

"Are you all right?" I asked, steadying the sixty-something woman nearest me. She pressed a hand to her forehead, and a moment passed.

"Wooo! He was great!" she shrieked, and pumped the air with her fist.

They all thanked the driver with big hugs and a generous tip.

"Now, ladies," he said, blushing, "Win a lot of money, meet a lot of men and have a beer for me."

They laughed and hurried into the lobby.

Security wandered away as Cowboy swaggered up to me, his eyes blazing. "Those dames was as fine as cream gravy," he told me. "Git me more jest like 'em, Jay." Then he gave me a hug that lifted me clear off the pavement.

"I will! I will!" I promised, laughing. "Now put me down!"

"Awright. Stay out of trouble my brother."

I watched his smoking cab blast off into the Vegas night.

"Come on, let's get a drink," T-bone said.

I was exhausted after my shift, but he insisted. His back had ruled out our going to the gym together. We hadn't found an opportunity to say more than a few words since our dinner in the cafeteria the week before.

I reluctantly accepted his invitation, thinking he might have changed his mind about talking to Sharkey . . . although I doubted it. "Okay. Let me just call home and let Cassy know."

I had remained loyal to T-bone after he let me down. I still considered him to be my friend, but only because my need to have friends was so huge. A part of me was feeling alone, and I needed to fill the void. Anyway, T-bone and I needed each other. The world at work was too chaotic and cold without being able to connect with someone nearby. Sam and Cassy were unavailable to me. Of the three, T-bone was the most accessible. (Some fucking basis for a friendship.) So I made excuses for his behavior: He's coughing. His sinuses are bothering him. He has stomach problems.

As we walked to his car in the employees' parking area, I called home on my cell. The answering machine picked up, and T-bone listened as I left a message.

"What, she sleeping or gone out?" he asked.

I shrugged.

"No one who's married should be out alone after ten o'clock."

"What am I supposed to do, give my wife a curfew?" I asked angrily.

"Of course not. What I'm saying is, if she's out after ten . . . well, you know how it can go. This town is crowded with assholes passing themselves off as nice guys. Most of them are fuckin' dicks! They're all a bunch of fucks!" T-bone's eyes were glazed, and he wasn't blinking. "If she's out after ten—"

"Jesus, Todd! Enough! I get the message!"

By ten, all the families were tucked safely into their suites, having enjoyed magic shows, amusement parks, and animal habitats. With the wholesome influence of the mommies, daddies, and children off the streets, Las Vegas took on an entirely different character, which became increasingly dark and salacious as the night ticked by. Any woman in the clubs during these hours was either on the prowl or was bait. Period.

When we got into his car, I confided what was going on with my marriage.

His mouth tightened, and he threw me a so-what-the-hell-did-you-expect? look. "Jay, you know Mary and I really like and trust you, man."

Jesus. "I know, Todd. I like and respect you, too. And Mary."

"And we respect your choices, you know? You're a smart guy, and I don't just mean that you have diplomas."

Where the fuck was he going with this?

"But we always thought Cassy was headed for trouble. She's been out of control for a long time, man."

He pulled into a little place off the Strip called The Freeway, an after-hours hangout for locals and people who worked the hotels. I'd never been there, but I'd heard it was a loud, busy, happening club. We passed shadowy forms standing in the darkness as we walked to the entrance. The area around the entry was packed with people coming and going. I'd rarely seen a place so obviously favored by locals. The noise spilled out into the parking lot—not just loud music but laughter and voices.

Even at two in the morning, everyone was in a party mood. T-bone had to raise his voice for me to hear him. "I went around and told all the hosts about our new sideline," he shouted. The hosts at the hotel were constantly in contact with the high rollers, many of whom loved Cuban cigars.

"Good," I screamed at his ear. "I spread the word around the cafeteria and with the valets."

Our coworkers knew people who would buy Cuban cigars. We weren't worried about getting caught. In Vegas customer service was many times more important than the law. Besides, we offered a finder's fee to our coworkers, so who would be dumb enough to turn us in? Even after subtracting a cut for the middleman, T-bone and I felt, we would do well.

Inside, The Freeway interior was dark, and my eyes had to adjust before I could join the action. The music was cranked at a loud level. We squeezed in at a U-shaped bar with built-in slot machines.

I greeted a few people I recognized from the Grand. Across from us sat one of our dealers from the casino, a good-looking, self-possessed guy with slicked-back black hair, wearing an Armani suit. I think his name was Ricardo. I was amazed to see him at The Freeway, of all places. I had expected him to hang out at one of the town's classy venues—a dance club in one of the casinos or a place with a lounge act. Maybe Studio 54 at the MGM, or the Voodoo Lounge at the Rio, or The Foundation Room at Mandalay. I watched as he played the slots.

I turned to point him out to T-bone, but my friend was surrounded by three guys patting him on the back and a trio of girls draped all over his neck and shoulders. I stared, speechless. T-bone claimed he headed to the gym or straight home after work. When his back pain ruled out the gym, he went home to soak in a hot bath. Obviously he was a regular at The Freeway. My partner, my *friend,* had never even mentioned the place to me!

"Hey, Todd-man!" The bartender smacked a shot glass of vodka down at T-bone's place, then he put a napkin in front of me and took my order.

T-bone leaned over and slung an arm around my shoulders. I was too surprised to say anything, and he quickly filled the void by returning to the discussion about my wife. "Listen. One time we went dancing and you had to go the bathroom? Some asshole asked Cassy to dance. . ." He paused, uncertain.

"Go on."

"All she had to do was smile and say, 'No, thanks, my husband wouldn't like it,' ya know? Instead she ignored him. So he asked again, and she told him to get lost." He spread his hands, palms up. "Why create an enemy for nothin'? If he'd been drunk enough, things would've gotten ugly, for no good reason."

My stomach was in a knot. I didn't want to hear any more, but Todd was just warming up. "When Cassy is out of control, she's not dependable. She's bitten my head off, and Mary's and yours, for no good reason. She acts like she's having this great time, but she's always so pissy and sarcastic, I have to wonder what the fuck is really going on in her head."

I stared into my mug as my anger grew. He was right, but who the hell was he to be pointing fingers? What kind of secret life did *he* have going on?

"She gets that hard look when she drinks and smokes a lot. Her appearance and the way she acts—" he shrugged "—they don't make you think she's off-limits."

I nodded. Cassy's whole demeanor invited assumptions. In some towns—L.A., for instance—that would have been inconsequential. A man would look at a beautiful woman and say, "She's hot. Maybe she's an actress." In Vegas, men would assume that same woman was a showgirl, a dancer in a topless club, or a hooker. A lot of women alternated among all three jobs. That's exactly why these beauties had come to Vegas. Men could reasonably expect a warm reception when they approached with an offer to buy a lady a drink. Cassy's appearance broadcast an open invitation, but then she rejected her suitors. Of course a guy would feel manipulated and pissed off.

"Like she's so seductive," T-bone continued, "but then if some dude puts his hand on her ass, she's screaming, 'I didn't do anything! It's his fault!' If she springs that on the wrong guy, she'll end up in a lot of shit. And with your temper Jay, it would get ugly. You know what I'm saying?"

"You think I don't know that? But I can't get through to her."

T-bone shook his head. "I feel for ya, man."

I sat in glum silence, thinking how much worse the situation might become with Cassy acting that way.

"So you like this place?" Todd asked brightly. "You figured out yet what the deal is here?"

"No. What?"

He nodded discreetly toward the dealer from the Grand. "Pay attention."

The bartender approached Ricardo, who dropped a few bills into the metal coin tray of the slot machine. I figured he was digging for change. What happened next unfolded with such speed, I wouldn't have caught it if T-bone hadn't prepared me. With one slick move, the bartender swept up the bills and deposited a little plastic bag in its place, which Ricardo quickly covered with his hand and transferred into his jacket pocket. Then he casually stood, settled his bar bill, and was on his way. Less than a minute later, an attractive blonde took his place. As I watched, the bartender surreptitiously completed another transaction.

"That bartender's selling blow!" I said to T-bone.

"Ain't just the bartender," he confided. "This place is run by the Chinese mafia. That's why people come here."

Once T-bone explained the system, I took in how many people were arriving, doing business at the bar, and then leaving. The Freeway should have had a revolving door. The place was a zoo. Not all the activity was handled discreetly, either. In my opinion, some of the sellers and buyers were acting as if their commodity was as benign as laundry detergent.

I felt vulnerable and uneasy. The Grand was very strict about having drug-free employees. Anyone caught "partaking" would get their ass fired immediately. The corporation took advantage of every legal opportunity to test us for drugs. If we had to fill out an accident report, for example, the nurse passed us a plastic cup as soon as our injury was treated and told us to leave a urine sample behind.

As I scanned the crowd, I wondered how many shadowy forms masked by the darkness recognized me? How many knew my name? Who among them would gladly offer my head on a platter to Sharkey or Bug-eyed Dick?

Why am I even here? I asked myself. I had to be the most naive person in the room! I felt shaky with self-loathing, and I was pissed off at my partner for being the dumbest guy at The Freeway. If he wanted to stick himself in a risky situation, fine. But how the hell could he have brought me along without first explaining what the place was about? And how could we be such good buddies with his keeping this hangout a secret from me?

I stared at him while shooting down the last of my drink. "Todd, I don't know who the fuck you are."

He looked startled. "C'mon," he said. "Let's get out of here." He settled up with the bartender, and we forged our way outside.

We could not have left fast enough for me; local, state, and federal authorities took drug trafficking very seriously. Back in the early sixties, Attorney General Robert Kennedy raided every important casino in Las Vegas and Reno and raised a constitutional uproar. Governor Grant Sawyer, an extremely popular Democrat, knew that Kennedy could not possibly be basing his coordinated raids on probable cause—that agents were likely to find evidence of criminal conduct at every casino.

The governor perceived Kennedy's scheme as a public-relations stunt, to create the image of a tough, aggressive lawman. Sawyer wanted none of it. He felt the attorney general was casting such a wide net, it would catch the innocent as well as the guilty and have a terrible effect on tourism. Sawyer decided to tell him so . . . in person. The governor had campaigned in behalf of John Kennedy's bid for president the year before.

The meeting in Washington did not go well. The governor came away feeling Robert Kennedy had treated him disrespectfully and had implied Sawyer was connected to the mob.

The next day Governor Sawyer took himself to the White House and the Oval Office, where he described to President John Kennedy the steps lawmakers had already taken to clean up the state. Apparently he made his point. The raids were canceled. But if the police heard that the Chinese mafia had taken over The Freeway and turned cocaine into an over-the-counter drug, the force certainly had the place under surveillance.

Once T-bone and I were in the parking lot, he pulled out a small plastic bag filled with coke. I hadn't even seen him make the buy. He stopped in the middle of the blacktop, threw back his head, and took a hit.

"What the fuck are you doing?" I asked, looking around for agents and cameras.

He offered me the bag as he vacuumed air through his nostrils. "Whaddaya mean?"

"If someone from work saw you do that, you'd lose your fucking job—and take me down with you." I pointed back at the building. "I mean, that could've been a disaster for both of us! How many times, man, are you going to hang my ass off the edge of a cliff and think it's no big deal?"

"It's okay!" he assured me with coke-induced confidence. "Would you please chill?" He held out the bag for me again.

"No!" I said, feeling very angry.

"What is your problem, man? No one is going to say a word. Everyone in there is doing the same shit," he said, getting into the car.

"Asshole, a narc could get lost in that crowd very easily. You don't know who's there or why."

"Jay. Please. Don't fuck up my buzz."

I stood in the parking lot and fumed. It was all about him. As usual. Whenever our friendship required a compromise or concession, I was always the one to make it. Being friends with T-bone demanded energy, time, effort, and stamina.

So why did I put up with him? He was so self-involved, he didn't have much left over for a friendship, but he loved and respected me in his own limited way. He believed we were friends. He always made a big deal of how much he trusted me and how I could rely on him. What Todd represented, as shitty as it turned out to be, I needed.

I'd always had close friends until I got to Vegas. I fell in with T-bone right away and assumed he could deliver on his offer to watch my back. He seemed crazy but fun and genuine. His obsession with health foods and supplements was annoying at first, but it didn't have that much impact on my existence.

Yes, he lived his life at the speed of sound, but I could accept his being so hyper, because we were an amazing team at the hotel, and he was an incredible training buddy at the gym.

I respected his choice of life's partner—a smart woman born to anchor him. The two couples going out together had been great fun. When that ended, Mary and T-bone came over to the house while Cassy was at work. We three got high and listened to music and talked for hours. Those afternoons meant a lot to me.

I supposed if I had realized how limited T-bone's friendship would eventually prove, I would have continued to search for a buddy. That wasn't how things played out, though. At this point, I felt that T-bone was who he was, and I simply accepted him and what he had to give me. His dependence on painkillers concerned me, as did his need to use uppers to balance out the depressants. I was even handling his refusal to admit his role in Sharkey's comeuppance.

What I could not accept was not trusting him.

Less than an hour before, he'd said that when Cassy was out of control, she wasn't trustworthy. As far as I could tell, the only difference between T-bone and Cassy was that I had already known the many ways Todd was a loose cannon; I was just finding out about Cassy.

Now he started the car, and the backup lights came on as I stood still on the blacktop, trying to gain some perspective. So big fucking deal, I told myself. He's taken an unnecessary risk. Nobody's perfect. Doing coke in the middle of a parking lot was no big deal. Everyone was doing it, right?

Whatever, my rage came with me into the passenger seat. While T-bone drove me back to the Grand, I slumped in the darkness. I had an ominous feeling about this secret side taking him down.

How much more disappointment and bullshit was I willing to swallow?

In this town, when someone found a friend he loved—or even liked—he wanted to hold on. Making friends in Vegas was so tough, T-bone and I, and Sam and I, made a point of discussing trust, so we would never lose sight of what we needed from each other. This became an integral part of our relationship. We always made sure we were on the same page because of the place we worked in.

When I first started working at the hotel, I tried to strike up a conversation with one of the other trainees, a guy who had worked in other hotels. He shut me down fast. "I never make friends where I work," he told me, "and if you're smart, you won't, either. You can't trust anyone."

I had felt sorry for him then. Now experience was teaching me he was right, and the proof was driven home hard at The Freeway.

Maybe in part, Cassy was right. I had learned what being abandoned and alone felt like at too young an age. As a kid, I reacted to my feelings with anger. These had been my core issues—and my demons—from childhood. I have to feel connected to someone. Nothing could soothe my wounds when these needs weren't met.

My demons came roaring to life in Vegas. My worst nightmares had become reality: simultaneously losing my wife and my friend Sam and now this shit with T-bone. The possibility of losing my job. I struggled with the demons, but they were winning the battle and tearing me down emotionally and physically.

Was I so different from anyone else in the world? Everyone needed love—more than was possible to get. Cassy and T-bone's emptiness was so huge, they treated it with alcohol or drugs and denial. Their true self was buried so deep, they had lost their way. I couldn't access it anymore, either, and I didn't know who the hell I was talking to during our conversations.

But we all had choices. Mine were right in front of me. I had to decide if a shitty friendship was better than no friendship at all, and if having an estranged spouse was preferable to being single. I honestly didn't know. I could continue to try to fill the void, no matter what the cost to my peace of mind, or I could face my worst fear and feel the agony of being alone.

CHAPTER Twelve

The man responsible for transforming Las Vegas from a nowhere town in the Nevada desert into the gambling power plant of North America was Benjamin Hyman Siegelbaum. He built the city's first resort casino, the Flamingo, and in the process won a place in American history.

Ironically, the casino that made his reputation also, "caused him to be murdered by contractual agreement." Benjamin Siegelbaum, better known as Bugsy Siegel, evidently foolishly skimmed money from his investors and stashed it in numbered Swiss bank accounts. When the Syndicate found out, it assigned Bugsy's murder to one of its contractors, who carried out the mission June 20, 1947, while Bugsy was relaxing at home, reading a newspaper.

The need for such measures at the executive level was unusual. Las Vegas's founding fathers strictly observed a code of honor in business, and they treated all guests with the kind of respect absent today. I witnessed this firsthand back in the seventies, when I visited my uncle who was a big player at the

Sahara Hotel. He always stayed in the Presidential Suite on the top floor. Inside the elevator, instead of pushing a button, my uncle used a key to get to his room.

In the middle of the suite's dining-room table, a huge crystal bowl brimmed with shrimp, crab, and lobster on ice, compliments of the hotel. I had never before seen such a gift, in all its crustaceous grandeur. The management had made certain that bottles of Archie's favorite twenty-year-old Scotch filled his wet bar.

Were any detail overlooked, my uncle could call upon his private butler twenty-four hours a day. But I wondered what they could possibly have forgotten? I wondered, after discovering matchbooks embossed with my uncle's initials and four thick terrycloth robes, all monogrammed, in his bathroom. A carton of Parliaments, his favorite cigarette, sat on his night table. As far as I could tell, someone had thought of everything.

This exceptional service extended beyond the confines of Uncle Archie's suite. He had a standing invitation for complimentary meals at any of the hotel's restaurants and for any of the Sahara's services, as well as comp tickets to any show in town. The bell captains, pit bosses, and members of management would have done anything he wanted. Anything. Of course my uncle, in reality, paid for all of this and more on the crap table.

One year I had a problem getting a flight home because all the airlines were booked. Archie walked me to the bell captain's desk and explained my dilemma. The captain smoothly dialed an outside line, and within a couple of minutes the airline had bumped a passenger from the flight and given me the seat.

Uncle Archie put his hand on my shoulder and guided me from the captain's desk. "The next time you come into town," he said quietly into my ear, "be sure to bring the bell captain a nice bottle of red wine as a thank-you. You *always* repay a favor. It shows you got some class."

Ah, those were the days. Jazz in the casino lounges. Sinatra in the big room. Sport jackets and chiffon scarves. Tuxedos and long gowns. Deferential, preferential treatment.

By the time I moved to Las Vegas, the original Italian good ol' boys were long gone, but I worked with some of their sons and grandsons. Hotel chains and corporations had supplanted the Syndicate. The Hilton Corporation purchased Bugsy's Flamingo Hotel, and with sweeping symbolism, wrecking balls demolished his private bungalow with its three-inch-thick concrete walls.

People who had enjoyed Vegas in the fifties, sixties, and seventies believed the city had now grown too corporate, too big, too greedy. The bottom line had to look good to the share-holders, so rather than catering to the individual, most hotels tried to capture the hordes. Now each guest was a "potential profit center"; his room, food, and drink were "revenue."

I saw other ways in which Las Vegas had not changed at all. Since the 1940s the desert oasis seemed to bedevil everyone who spent time there with a black magic that was both subtle and utterly transmuting. I could best describe the city's witchery as a force field, an electric undercurrent. I felt it vibrating beneath the pavement on the Strip.

Manifesting as light and heat and sound, its charge and frequency proved toxic to some people but not to others. I guessed its ultimate impact depended upon each individual's neurochemistry, experience, and length of exposure to the force field's electromagnetic oscillations. If you felt its heat, saw its light, and heard its beckoning song, it would scramble your brain, just like electroshock treatment.

I was lucky. During my first weeks as a doorman, the electri-cal current under the Strip energized me. I stayed strong and focused. All around me, though, people gave off a vapor of portending doom. Cassy. Sam. T-bone. Mary. The vibronics had plugged into their brain, bonded with the receptors, rewired the circuitry, and eventually burned them alive.

When I had begun my job on the Strip, I was a wide-eyed recruit. The stories passed around about the guests' or staffs' sexual escapades shocked me . . . until I began to feel the effect of the city's insidious electrical current. I changed. I became so jaded, the only stories I found shocking described someone living a clean life.

One night I realized I, too, gave off the odor of moral collapse. I was terrified. What if I couldn't scrub off the stench? What if my thighs permanently bore the dark stains of dollar bills stuffed into my uniform pockets? I wanted to be cleansed and exorcized of the monsters that were taking hold of my state of mind.

As soon as I got home, I showered with the hottest water I could tolerate. I scoured my body and my hands and sucked the suds up into my nostrils to rid myself of the foul smell. But I couldn't get away from it; I was becoming a part of the darkness.

"This will be your first fight night, Jay?" the Professor asked me.

We were in the locker room, changing clothes. I was getting into my uniform, and the Professor had just finished his shift.

"That's right. Have any words of wisdom?"

"Always," he replied, a twinkle in his eyes. "But are you referring specifically to fight night?"

I just rolled my eyes at his sense of humor.

"I don't want to alarm you, but not a Rolling Stones concert, not the COMDEX convention, and not even the National Rodeo Finals will come close to what you're going to witness tomorrow tonight."

"How can it be worse than New Year's Eve, Professor?" Now I really had no idea what to expect.

"In every possible way." He tied the laces on his suede shoes, straightened, and looked me in the eyes. "If you want to clock in on time, I suggest you leave your house a couple hours earlier than usual."

I studied the man for a moment, trying to decide if he were catastrophizing or playing a joke. I decided he was on the level. The Professor and I hadn't spent much time talking, but when I'd mentioned thinking Bug-eyed Dick was a good guy, the Professor had not exactly agreed. He'd also pointed out how I'd inadvertently invited Weasel to make a fool of me in public. That was two for two.

"I defer to your wisdom, O great one," I said.

He laughed, shaking his head, as he grabbed his duffel bag. "Vegas and boxing have been so paired in people's conscious-ness, the general population would be amazed to learn that the city's first match wasn't until 1961. June 26, to be exact, at the convention center."

"Would I be familiar with the boxers?"

"Oh, yeah. Cassius Clay, at that time just a kid from Louisville—"

"No shit!"

"No, none that I know of," he said a bit distastefully. "His opponent was Duke Sabedong, from Hawaii."

I searched my brain. "Did he have a reputation for fighting dirty?"

"The very one. But it was a good match. Sabedong was big, strong, and experienced. Clay was considered one of the best kids on the way up. Sabedong landed a punch below the belt, but Clay was too fast and skillful to be beaten. The bout was over pretty quickly."

I thanked the Professor and told him about meeting Joe Louis, and then he exited to the baggage room, passing a couple of valets, pals of Dick's, on the way in.

"Hey," I said, by way of greeting.

"Hey," they responded unenthusiastically, and walked along the benches, end to end in the center aisle, until they came to their lockers.

"You guys ready for the fight?" I asked them.

They looked at me dully.

"I've heard that nothing pulls in more people than a championship boxing match," I continued.

The boys barely glanced at me as they shrugged off their uniforms.

What the fuck was that about? I wondered, and suddenly realized none of Dick's little buddies was talking to me. Did they hold me responsible for Dick's run-in with HR at Christmastime? If they did, they were morons. He still occupied a supervisory position, even after being disciplined by Mrs. Levine in HR for hanging Christmas decorations and posting his church's holiday-sermons schedule in his office.

I went downstairs and through the lobby on my way to the porte cochere. A gigantic banner strung above me proclaimed: *HE'S BACK!* I guessed the Grand's Marketing Department had given that a lot of thought. "He" was Mike Tyson, who had converted to Islam while in prison and changed his name. But if the banner had read: *MALIK ABDUL AZIZ IS BACK!* would anyone have cared?

I wasn't a fan of Tyson even though I believed he was one of the best heavyweights who ever lived. My only interest in Tyson was how much money I'd make as a result of his name on the marquee.

He'd sat in an Indiana prison for three years, having been found guilty of raping a beauty-pageant contestant. The boxer claimed he was innocent because the young woman had gone willingly to his hotel room. Her naïveté did not let him off the hook. As far as I was concerned, he was a bad man, maybe the baddest man on the planet coming to fight at my hotel, in a town starving for his comeback.

"Yo," T-bone called, and walked over to me. "Tyson and McNeeley, heh?" Todd had been very chummy since our little scene at The Freeway a couple nights before. "It's fucked, man. No fucking way is McNeeley a top-ten contender. King must've screwed around with McNeeley's stats. *I* wouldn't want to be facing Tyson, I know that."

A long black limo pulled up to where T-bone and I were standing, and I moved forward to open the door.

"You fucked a hooker!" the woman in the backseat screamed.

The limo driver walked around and rolled his eyes at me and T-bone as the three of us stood waiting for the passengers to vacate the limo.

"I didn't screw her," the man said under his breath. He looked deeply pained as he and the woman climbed out of the car and walked toward the lobby doors.

"Well, then!" she shrieked, indignant. "I guess a blow job is okay, you fucking idiot!"

They disappeared into the lobby, and the limo driver sped away.

T-bone guffawed. "Busted!" He seemed to be enjoying what had just happened.

"You think that's funny?" I asked, incredulous. Just as at The Freeway, I stared at Todd and thought, I don't know who the fuck you are.

The same couple suddenly exploded out through the lobby doors. They were arguing hotly, and T-bone stepped back, no longer smiling, as the man waved for his own cab. I decided to leave them alone, too. They both looked dangerously pissed off.

"You went out of control!" she yelled, jabbing her finger toward her husband's chest.

"Oh, shut the fuck up, why don't you!" he yelled back, and gestured again for the cab. The woman looked stunned.

I knew the script. I had heard it all before, and I'd be hearing it again, probably before the weekend was over. Next she would burst into tears and lock herself in their room. He'd go out and get very, very drunk.

On cue, the woman burst into tears and ran back toward the lobby as the man slammed the taxi's door behind him and disappeared into the night.

T-bone and I stood at the curb in silence. I was only about ten minutes into my work shift.

"Let's hope we're just getting all the crap outta the way now, and it ain't gonna go on like this all night," he said.

We watched the lobby doors warily. The next person to emerge was one of the casino hosts, his hand on the elbow of one of our guests.

"Please call a cab to take Mr. Yashi to the airport," the host said to T-bone.

Piccolo Pete pulled up, and we watched them drive off.

"Big player?" I asked.

The host nodded. "But he lost everything. Couldn't even afford taxi fare to the airport."

"So is Pete gonna take a hit for the fare?" I asked.

The host shook his head. "The hotel gave Mr. Yashi a few hundred dollars so he could get back to Japan."

"How much did he lose?" I asked as the host turned to go back inside.

"Close to a million dollars," he called back to us, and grinned.

"Aw, Jesus!" T-bone said to me. "How could anyone be that stupid? I mean, you have to know when the fuck to stop!"

"Do *you* know?" I asked him under my breath.

A movie came to mind, unbidden. In it, Nick Nolte starred as an aging football hero whose body had fallen apart from all the hard hits he had taken throughout his career. Next I thought of Cassius Clay, the best boxer the world had ever seen. In his glory days he had danced around the ring, throwing jabs and knockout punches and giving his opponents lip. Now he could barely talk or move.

T-bone reminded me of them. He had been such a bull and so full of energy just a few months before. Now I was witnessing the disintegration of his body, mind, and spirit. Joe Louis had died in a wheelchair, and probably Todd would, too.

Is this what his wife had feared? That Todd would not know when to stop numbing his back pain with drugs and alcohol, so I would need to be his nursemaid? How the hell was I supposed to do that? I could hardly have a conversation with him, and I was growing so disgusted with the man he was proving himself to be, I didn't want to take him on as my project.

"Hey, you! Get me a fucking cab."

I looked up to see a man heading directly at me from the lobby. His overcoat was unbuttoned, flapping behind him, and his necktie was askew. I instinctively looked directly into his eyes. They were swollen and red.

"Now, asshole!" he demanded.

I tensed but kept my cool. "Excuse me, sir, I will. Just calm down."

"Don't fucking tell me to calm down! Get me the cab!"

I waved for the first cab in line. The Candy Lady.

"Open the fucking door for me, scumbag!" He stared with rage directly into my eyes.

I wanted to break him in half, right then and there. I saw myself doing it, and for a split second I felt myself doing it. Fortunately the Candy Lady drove up in time to stop me. I opened the door, and the man hurled himself into the back. Then he turned and flicked his cigarette at my crotch.

The Candy Lady gasped, looking at her fare in the rearview mirror. She stopped bouncing in her seat and put the car into gear. For the first time, she did not try to toss me a piece of candy as she took off.

T-bone walked over in disgust and stepped on the smoking butt, then pitched it in the trash. "They say putting up with this crap makes us stronger."

"Bullshit!" I was so angry, I could hardly speak. "It makes us weaker." I brushed the ashes off my uniform. Again. "It chips away at my self-worth and makes me softer." I looked up at him. "How many times am I going to have some drunken stranger in my face? How many times do I have to stand here while some bottom feeder takes potshots at me? How many times have I stood here thinking how badly I want to hurt this person but having to swallow my rage?"

"I know, buddy. I know."

"Do you, Todd?" I fumed. "Do you know that when I get home in the middle of the night, I have to beat the heavy bag hanging in my garage until my knuckles bleed, just to get some of the anger out of my system so I can go to sleep? How long before this shit makes me sick?"

"Maybe we could get some blow and—"

"*No!*" I shouted.

His eyes widened.

"I'm not going to do painkillers or beta blockers or double shots or anything else that's going to numb me out and then kill me!" Tears burned my eyes. "I can't be like everyone else, Todd.

I won't be that stupid. I'm better than that and smarter. I have to be smart enough to know when to quit."

T-bone laughed at me. I couldn't believe it, but he actually fucking laughed. "This town isn't about being smart," he said lightly. "Don't try to think in Vegas, man. It'll only slow you down."

Fight night. Thank you, Professor: As he had predicted, the twenty-minute drive to work took me well over two hours because nothing on the Strip moved. Tropicana Boulevard was packed to capacity. I circled the city to find a different route into the hotel, but every square inch of road was taken, and no alternatives existed.

If I thought the hotel had been a zoo on New Year's Eve, then fight night could only be described as ten zoos. I withdrew inside myself for protection from the all-out chaos. Using automatic pilot, I made my way through the throngs and eventually came to the front of the cab line. At first I found the maximum overload of Vegas sights and sounds thrilling. So many people streaming into the Grand's lobby reminded me of Super Bowl fans surging into a sold-out stadium.

And then they vanished.

The porte cochere became quiet.

I glanced toward the staging area. Very few cabs waited there. We'd need a shitload more vehicles, with the city so full. I hoped they would be ready when we needed them.

"You look like crap."

I turned to see T-bone at my shoulder.

We stood together and talked about nothing. By his glazed eyes I could see he was jacked up, and I was preoccupied by our sparse cab line. What did the drivers know that I didn't? The city was jammed, yes, but not everyone could have gotten a ticket to the bout. So where were they? I had hoped we would make good money on fight night, but now I wasn't so sure.

Disgusted, I turned to my partner. "I'm going to get something to eat. Now seems like good timing . . ."

"I'll come with you," he said, and asked one of the valets to watch the line for us.

We walked along the corridor to the cafeteria.

"What the hell are you two doing, leaving your posts on a night like this?"

Sharkey came running toward us. He was pissed. I was not about to open my mouth.

"Boss, it's quiet out there," T-bone explained. "We won't have a chance to eat after the fight lets out, so—"

He glanced at his diver's watch. "You have exactly twenty minutes! If you're not back at your station, you're fired! Do I make myself clear?"

"Yes, sir," we said in unison, and then, as we walked away, we both whispered, "asshole."

Sharkey meant what he said, so we didn't bother finding a place to sit down. We rushed through the carry-out cases and helped ourselves without focusing on our choices. I shoved a ham salad on wheat down my throat, followed by a too-sweet pint of tropical punch, even as we jogged back to the cab line. The area was empty.

"I don't know why we had to be in such a fucking hurry," T-bone groused, eyeing his turkey on white with mayonnaise. "The fight must've just started."

"It's over! It's over!" A bellboy burst through the lobby doors, screaming the news. His face was flushed with excitement. "Tyson needed less than two minutes!" The kid shook his fists above his head and did a little dance. "He's back!" he shrieked. "He's back!"

Seconds later the porte cochere resembled Red Square on May Day. The temperature rose, and the air became congested with smoke—cigars, cigarettes, and marijuana. I tried to take deep breaths to get enough oxygen from somewhere in that potent mix.

The taxi line took on monstrous dimensions, snaking down the side of hotel and out of sight along Tropicana Boulevard. Still, we ran out of cabs and limos. Already T-bone was barking into his cell phone, begging every cab company in town for immediate help. He came back to me, shaking his head.

"What's wrong?" I asked.

"The motherfuckin' cabs and limos are stuck in gridlock on the Strip," he said. "They're tryin' to get here, but they can't."

We turned around to look at the people, thousands and thousands of them, like so many snowflakes in a blizzard, all waiting for T-bone and me to hand them into a cab. I turned away, nervous they would read my body language and start a riot. T and I would be torn limb from limb.

The tension built as the two cultures heaved and swayed into each other—the blacks well above the radar and the whites well below the radar. The police came out in force. Drug dealers were everywhere; I believe they were exponentially building their retirement fund and probably thinking in concrete terms of Tahiti. A lot of hookers worked the crowd and served as the throng's only distraction.

And then the gathering began to grasp the situation: Cabs were few, and if the people did not want to stand in the cab line all night, they would need to take action. And so the money came out. Twenties replaced dollar bills. Then hundred dollar bills replaced the twenties. People were shoving money at T-bone and me.

"We need a plan!" he said breathlessly. "I'll take the hundred-dollar people off to the side of the cab line. You stay with the line. As the cabs come in, send every third one my way. Okay?"

"Got it. Go."

When I had a moment, I looked over at T-bone. At least a hundred people surrounded him, and he was taking in a lot of money. His plan worked, but for only so long.

The crowds grew larger and more congested. Some folks, their blood already running hot from their just having seen a boxing match, became angry and tried to cut in front of everyone else. Fights broke out. Bottles flew end over end. The police were arresting people as fast as they could.

"Jay!" a woman's voice called out.

I located the twenty-something female in the crowd. She didn't look familiar, but she did look drunk. I guessed she read my name tag.

"Jay? Oh, Jay," she called in a singsong voice. "I have something for you if you'll get me out of here." And then, right in front of the whole world, she pulled a huge plastic penis from her purse and slid it into her mouth. "Right here, Jay! Right now!"

She demanded that I drop my lion-tamer pants, and a group of black men surrounded us.

"When I'm done with you, Jay," she promised melodiously, "you'll get a limo for me and my crew, right?"

"You will need to get in line and wait your turn if you want to leave," I told her.

"Fuck that!" the dildo queen shrieked.

Security moved in, and within seconds a fight erupted on the sidewalk. Police converged from nowhere and handcuffed the harridan and her crew and took them away. I continued working.

And working. As the night wore on, I lost my voice. I was dehydrated but couldn't take a moment for something to drink.

"My pockets can't hold another bill."

"What?"

T-bone was at my shoulder. I looked down at his uniform trousers pockets. They were bulging to such an extent, they looked bizarre.

"I'll be right back." Not missing a beat, Todd ran between two parked cars, bent down to minimize his profile, and emptied his pockets into his hat.

Oh, shit, I thought. I didn't want to think what would happen if a stiff breeze blew his hat off and released the money into the crowd.

I glanced at my watch: four-thirty. The sun would be coming up in an hour. The cab line was still a hundred yards long, but at least the vehicles were finally flowing in.

T-bone approached, staggering a bit and looking dazed.

"Todd, you go inside and start to count the money. I'll watch the line." I knew counting that much cash and splitting what we had earned that night would take awhile.

He nodded and went inside.

As the sun rose, T-bone returned, holding out a thick envelope.

"Already divided?" I asked.

He nodded tiredly. "That's yours."

"How much?"

He grinned. "Two thousand each, buddy. Sweet dreams."

CHAPTER THIRTEEN

As the weeks went by, the screws tightened. My "partner" hardly deserved that description, he was so messed up on painkillers, sleeping pills and alcohol. He was in agony, and I took on as much of the heavy work as I could. . . on the nights T-bone felt well enough to show up.

Todd's sex life was nonexistent because of his back. His days at the gym were long gone. He began to drink more and more. No longer could he put off seeing a real doctor. He began making appointments with orthopedic surgeons, and they ordered diagnostic tests. Every time I spoke to him, he was meeting yet another back specialist, one after the other.

"So what did they do today, man?"

"Something called a *discogram*," he told me.

"What's that?"

"An enhanced X-ray of the discs between my vertebrae. Tomorrow I'm getting an *MRI—a* magnetic resonance—"

"I know what an MRI is, Todd. When will you get the results?"

"A couple of days, I hope. I'm going nuts here, with nothing to do."

He promised to call me with the diagnoses, but Mary placed the call while T-bone was asleep. "His condition is really serious." She sounded scared.

"So what do the doctors say?" I asked, knowing all too well that surgeons usually recommended surgery.

"All the doctors agreed that disc-fusion surgery will eventually leave Todd confined to a wheelchair—"

"Jesus."

"So they prescribed specific back exercises, along with stronger painkillers." She sniffed. "Todd can't accept that, Jay. How can they not be able to do anything for him?"

I felt shitty about it, but when Mary started to sob, I looked at my watch and cut the conversation short with a promise to call the next day. I told her I had to get to my post on time. I didn't tell her that I couldn't take on anyone else's drama at the moment.

Sharkey and the hotel's guests continued to threaten and berate us; Bug-eyed Dick and his boys acted as if I were the invisible man. As for my wife and Sam, I did not know where the hell they were or what the fuck they were doing.

My emotional state deteriorated into a thorny tangle of depression and agitation. Food lost its flavor, and my exhaustion never subsided. I couldn't tolerate bright lights. Colors faded to black and white. The eyes in the mirror were too dull and lifeless to pass judgment anymore. I was sensitive to noise, but paradoxically I needed to blast Metallica and AC/DC—aggressive, visceral music—in my car as I drove home from work.

To get my mind off my mind, I partied nonstop, then reported to work hung over and worn out. I stood at my workstation, surrounded by guests who appeared and acted the same way

I did. They probably felt as shitty, too. The worse I felt, the higher my anxiety level. I was probably heading off that cliff Bug-eyed Dick had warned me about. Funny thing: while he was witnessing my spiral toward disaster, I was watching his. Because he and I defined Armageddon so differently, we were oblivious to our own impending doom.

Like my friends and wife, Dick hurtled toward disaster by crossing lines and violating boundaries. He perceived the whole world as his ministry, and the Grand was one of his outreach programs. We were in Lent now, with Easter and Passover in a couple of weeks. On several occasions I walked into the employee locker room and caught Dick preaching to the young valets and bellboys. Dick's choice of location almost guaranteed disaster—now that Human Resources had warned him that mixing Church and the workplace was illegal, Mrs. Levine would certainly keep an eye on him. But if he wanted to get himself nailed, that was not my problem. In fact, I had been keeping my distance from him as much as possible.

Unfortunately my biological dad's eighty-third birthday party would be held in two weeks, and I wanted to be at the celebration. I couldn't pretend he'd be around forever and have more birthdays—or even one more—so I had no choice but to ask Dick for a change in my work schedule.

Even as I went looking for Dick before my shift began, I suspected my timing couldn't have been worse. My fundamentalist supervisor no doubt held all Jews responsible for his Savior's death. I felt I personally had had nothing to do it. As I opened the locker-room door, I heard Dick's voice, in its ministerial mode. He stood with the bell captains' glass-walled office at his back.

"To achieve greatness as followers of Jesus, we must make sacrifices, and instead of grieving the loss, we must feel the fullness of great joy in our heart.

I cleared my throat.

Startled, Dick looked up and found me standing behind him. The bell man he was speaking to quickly left. Dick slowly turned on his heels and went into his office and sat down at the desk, the schedule book open like a bible. His posture was ramrod straight. I followed him at a slow pace and stopped in the doorway.

He had always arranged these shift exchanges in the past, no questions, no big deal. Keeping my tone casual and friendly, I began, "Hey, Dick, my family is planning a special birthday party for my old man. Can we find someone to trade days off with me—"

"No, that doesn't seem possible." He gave the scheduling sheets a cursory glance.

I started. *"What?"*

Dick raised his eyebrows at me, as if I had dared to question his authority. "I said I don't see your trading a day off with another doorman as being possible."

"Why not?"

"It would disrupt the service we provide our guests, and it would inconvenience another doorman."

"Dick, he's old. Family is coming in from—"

"You have your answer." He closed the schedule book with an air of finality, set it aside, and gave his full attention to some other paperwork.

Rage balled my fists and locked my jaw. I stood still, but beyond the glass wall I saw his boys gravitating toward the office. Coming to watch the heathen sacrificed to the lion?

"What is it, Dick?" I asked, working my voice level. "We used to be okay with each other. Our whole relationship has changed. I want to know why."

"We never had a 'relationship,' Jay. You have requested a schedule change, and I have the authority to grant or deny it. I see nothing mysterious about that." He stood from his chair, his eyes never leaving my face. He kept the desk between us.

"It's more than that, and you know it," I said. "You used to let me take breaks when the nights were slow. Now you don't. I used to be able to come inside to get a drink of water. Now you won't let me. Tonight you say I can't go to my old man's eighty-third birthday party."

He spread his hands and shrugged. "That is my prerogative as your supervisor. Your asking for special favors does not guarantee I will grant them."

In that instant, my situation became blindingly clear: This was not a misunderstanding that Dick and I would be able to work out. No passage of time would soften his attitude toward me. Never again would our working relationship be smooth. From now on, for as long as I worked at the Grand with Dick as my supervisor, my requests would be denied. No matter if I wanted a glass of water or time off when the hotel was slow.

I would not be able to figure out a way to make things better by being a better employee, because our conflict had nothing to do with work or my job performance. It was all about religion. It was about my accepting Jesus Christ as my savior and my allowing Dick to show me the way. From now on, I would feel the stress of his rigid, unyielding, self-righteous enmity.

He had declared war on me, and as my supervisor, he wielded all the power and was assured of victory. Now that I was clear about where we stood with each other, I let go of all pretense and declared war right back on him.

I detonated. "What's got you so pissed off, Dick? Is it that I'm not conforming? Is my religion that upsetting to you?"

Dick backed up as I advanced on him. He was trapped against a counter along the wall.

"You haven't been 'born again,'" I shouted. "You're the same guy who fucked up so bad, you've fooled yourself into believing you could start your life over. But you've only stuck a bandage on your problems. You'd have been better off getting therapy than joining a church."

"You have to calm down!" he shrieked, and shielded his face with his hands.

"Don't you fuckin' tell me to calm down, you fuckin' hypocrite! Praying for forgiveness on Sunday doesn't mean you can be an asshole the rest of the week!" I advanced on him, ready to bash in his born-again brains. I would have done it, too, if four bellboys hadn't come on the run and jumped me.

"Don't touch me!" I shouted, throwing them off.

"Call HR!" Dick cried out. "Call Security!"

One of the boys flung himself at the phone.

I stormed from the office, through the baggage room, and down the corridor, muttering to myself, trying to cool down. I was glad the situation with Dick had reached a crisis. I decided to file a formal complaint with HR. Mrs. Levine was not one to let Dick violate hotel policy and federal law. Again.

I blasted out of the lobby doors to my workstation, where I took over the cab line. Standing there with my heart pumping, I tried to rationalize, compromise, and convince myself into believing my so-called father and his birthday party weren't that important. "Okay, so I won't be there," I grumbled. "How many of my fucking birthdays did he miss? Almost all of them."

Fuck it.

So what?

I don't care.

And all the other things I used to tell myself when I was a kid. But now my old man was not responsible for the fury burning inside me; it was caused by that piece of shit who thought I was on my way to hell.

Maybe he's right, I thought. But if he is, I swear I'll take his sorry ass down with me.

"I need a break," I told T-bone.

He snorted a laugh. "Already? You just got here, man."

"I don't mean literally. I need to lie down somewhere on a beach and not get up for three days. I'll have lots of food, drinks, and massages. . . ."

"Save a place for me," T-bone said, and slapped me on the back.

Just then I saw two security men escorting a guest out of the hotel. The fellow looked wobbly from too much alcohol and seemed not to present a threat.

"Get him a cab, will ya?" one of the guards asked me. He jabbed a thumb toward the lush. "That guy was talking to a slot machine."

I whistled up a cab. Cowboy was first in line, and I heard his engine wail. Oh, Jesus.

The men from security returned inside and left me with the guest. "So, how ya doing today, sir?" I asked him, keeping an eye on Cowboy's approach.

The guest tried to focus on me. "Have you ever heard of the guy in the slot machine?"

"What? What guy?"

"The guy in the slot machine," he answered with elaborate patience. "I'm telling ya, it's true—especially in this hotel. It ain't fair. There's someone in every machine who controls who wins."

"Oh, okay. You're telling me there's a real person inside all the slot machines, right?"

"That's right!" He seemed happy I understood. "I don't know how it's done. Maybe there's a control room somewhere. But I'm telling you, it's all controlled."

"*Mm,* I don't know about that." I tried a little logic. "That's a lot of people the hotel would have to hire."

Now he looked at me like I was an idiot. "They're all on commission, man!"

I remembered the research I had done, preparing for this job. "You know, I read a book once on slot machines, and it described winning and losing as 'the God in the machine.'"

"'The God in the machine'? Oh, no!" He was very distraught.

"Let me explain! The author meant that at any given second, literally hundreds of possible combinations exist. Until the arm is pulled or the button is pressed, there's no way of controlling the outcome. It's all luck and a little strategy."

He considered that for a moment. "Well, I never heard *that* before."

Cowboy roared up to the curb. He didn't jump it, but his tires scraped against the lip.

"Look, sir," I said, "go home, drink some water, and get some rest. I promise, nobody's inside our machines."

"Maybe nobody you know, but they're in there all right, and they can see you, too."

I opened the taxi door, and he banged his head climbing into the backseat.

As I watched Cowboy take off, I immediately began daydreaming about a beach, any beach, where I could lie down for a few days.

"Hey, goombah . . ."

I turned to see my buddy Paolo standing at my shoulder. He was a valet stationed right across the porte cochere from me. "Cowboy is a dude unto himself." He smiled.

Paolo and I shared a laugh, watching Cowboy's taxi swerve dangerously close to palm trees and decorative boulders in a landscaped island at the end of the driveway.

"Do you think that maniac will learn to drive before he runs over every visitor in the city?" Paolo asked.

"Probably not," I answered.

In some ways Paolo was a throwback to Vegas's early days. He had connections to the mob. I had found that most people believed anyone "connected" was in some ways a hero and a person to be respected. I personally found much to like about Paolo, not because he was connected but because he was a righteous guy, unlike most people I'd met. He was always genuine and a straight shooter whenever we had a chance to talk or hang out together.

A few high-class call girls worked for him. They were beautiful women, with expensive clothes and nice cars—the sort of ladies who never had to drum up business by strolling around the casino and looking available. Also on Paolo's payroll was Carmine, his buddy who had recently moved from the East Coast. While few would guess that Paolo was an Italian from New York or New Jersey, Carmine lacked none of the identifying, albeit stereotypical details: the dark turtleneck sweater under a sports jacket, the broad and enthusiastic gestures, the accent, the conspicuous gold-chain bracelet on his big-boned wrist, the black wraparound sunglasses.

"Jay, permit me the pleasure of introducing you to a couple of my friends?"

"Sure, Paolo."

He gestured toward the side of the driveway. My eyes settled on Carmine and two more guys, in their thirties, huge, thickly built. A nearby cluster of pygmy palms looked miniaturized by comparison. Paolo's friends closed the distance, shook hands with me. I didn't catch their names, and within moments they were gone, inside the hotel.

Paolo's eyes locked on mine. "Always remember," he said, jabbing an index finger into my heart, "you're like a brother to me."

"Thanks, Paolo. And you're like a brother to me."

He snorted, as if to say, *Listen to what I'm telling you.* "If I can ever take care of anything for you, you just let me know." He looked at me with meaning. "Anything."

Ah. Now I understood. I was touched . . . and a little surprised that he had already heard about my blowup downstairs in Dick's office.

"Thanks, man. I know you mean it," I said.

An offer of that nature in Las Vegas was not to be taken lightly. Certain people in the city already had every detail in place to set the plan in motion. People who did "jobs," whether collecting money or breaking someone's bones, would never go hungry in Vegas. Their services were considered an integral part of the city and its history. That was how things were handled.

"I think I have it under control, though," I added.

Paolo nodded, studying me. "If you change your mind, I have the resources at hand. Those boys are used to collecting debts . . . and not just money owed to the casino." He paused. "Many Neanderthal types try to pass here for human beings. They owe all manner of restitution. Good people deserve to reclaim what is rightfully theirs, and such is the case with you, Jay." He paused. "You might feel better if we take a chunk out of this 'Nick' piece of shit."

"Dick."

"What?"

"Dick. You mean Dick."

"No, I mean Nick. That bottom-feeder bartender at the Palms. His name is Nicky. We know all about this scumbag: where he lives, what he drives. Ya know, we found out he's married with a baby on the way. You believe this guy?" He punched me in the shoulder, a friendly gesture, but I was so ungrounded, I staggered sideways a couple of steps. Paolo thought I was kidding around, and he laughed appreciatively before he walked back toward his area.

Then he stopped and came back to me. "Guys like him need a lesson. You almost have to wait in line to take him out. My boys are pros, Jay. If you keep your mouth shut, Nick'll never know you gave the orders. Neither will Cassy."

The sound of the ocean roared in my ears, and for a moment I couldn't get my bearings. Then the darkness gave way to a whiteout—an icy desolation in my heart—and a penetrating whistle sent shooting pains through my eardrums.

"Okay?" Paolo asked.

"Yeah."

"I let you know, now you let me know." He gave me a hug, slapped me soundly on the back, then left me wobbling in the middle of the driveway. The planet had rocked off its axis, and beneath me, the pavement bucked and tilted. Nick? Who the fuck was Nick? I took a deep breath, then another. Nick . . . Cassy. Some fucking bartender and my fucking wife. As I got myself grounded, the taste of blood was in my mouth.

The city seemed massive to visitors and newcomers, but Vegas was a small town, really, and Cassy was always being watched—we all were. Friends looked out for us. Enemies collected evidence to use against us. Paolo's offer came to me out of love. Of course Vegas's love was like no other: it wore a mask of deceit, illusion, greed, and, in its own way, loyalty. For me, in this town, loyalty *was* love.

Thoughts of revenge gnawed at me all night. I was so tempted to give Paolo the nod. Why not? His guys knew what they were doing. I had confidence they would be effective and subtle. They probably broke arms more often than they killed people. One issue held me back. If I told Paolo to go ahead, this fuck, Nick, would not get his lesson for a month or, more likely, a year. Could I be patient enough to wait, or would I go after him, half-cocked and half-crocked, for the pleasure of smashing his face in myself?

Hiring soldiers—with a verbal agreement, never a written contract—required patience. They moved slowly, waiting until all hard feelings seemed to have healed after a dispute. I thought of it as "refrigerated revenge," for only when everyone had cooled off would the thugs mount their assault. Catching the victim off guard made the attack easy and, probably for some, fun. The wait also protected whoever had paid for the job. Anyone known to carry a grudge against the victim would be the logical suspect.

I'd heard stories of how a couple of enforcers traveled from Las Vegas to some unsuspecting schmuck's home in the Midwest or Southeast, say, and staked out the place until the whole family was home. Then the "boys" rang the doorbell. Usually the wife answered.

"We would like to see your husband privately," they'd say.

Once the strangers had entered the house, the deadbeat high roller realized how vulnerable he and his loved ones were. He and the visitors would retire to a den or family room. "You owe the casino sixty thousand dollars," the big men would say. "We're here to settle the account. Time is of the essence because for a year you've promised the check was in the mail. We don't want to come here again."

Almost without exception, the debtor would take out his checkbook, hand over a check for the full amount owed, and consider himself very lucky as he hastily escorted the men to the door and locked it behind them.

An interaction of this sort was dubbed the "Vegas Way." It was neat, clean, careful. But Nick, the bartender wouldn't be able to scribble a bank check to compensate me. How would Carmine put a price on my wife's fidelity? Was Cassy worth a broken arm and two legs? As for our marriage, would a broken kneecap and all of Nick's teeth be compensation? I could not wrap my mind around these thoughts.

Much easier to consider was the likelihood of my keeping a cool head and closed mouth until Paolo's people took care of Nick. The odds weren't good. I felt too disrespected. Before they got to Nick, I would hurt him, and Cassy, and probably myself, too, while I was at it. That was the sure thing. I just had to figure out what form my revenge would take.

CHAPTER FOURTEEN

It was a cold, early spring night, with a wind chill of thirty-four degrees. I felt as if I had ice on my face. The long cab line moved slowly. The fifty or so people were dressed for casinos, restaurants, and concerts—not for a porte cochere wind tunnel.

"Where you headed?" I asked the next person in line.

The guest gathered his vocabulary. "Yes. We need several stops to make. Is okay with driver?"

"Of course." I raised my hand for a cab. "Which hotels?"

"The first—how you say? Big fire."

"I beg your pardon?"

"Yes. The place of Ziggy and Ray, please. I don't pronounce good. Ziggy and—oh! Siegafried and Roy."

"That's the Mirage, sir. Where else would you like to go?" A disheveled, unshaven cabbie pulled up and leaned out his window to listen.

"The Dreidl, please."

"Where?" the driver asked, squinting.

"Yes. I am sorry. The big light. *'Pow!'*" He threw his arms wide and knocked my hat off my head. "The Lexus?"

T-bone limped over and went out of control with laughter. "Would that be the two-door or four-door?" he managed to ask as I picked up my hat. Laughter was odd for him these days, but possibly he was high on painkillers. "Yes, sir," I said. "That's the *Luxor* Hotel. Have a good time." While I helped the family into the backseat, the driver guffawed, smacking the steering wheel with the heel of his hand.

"Hey, man, I'm going inside to warm up." T-bone was blowing on his hands as he went through the hotel door.

"Yeah, go ahead," I told him.

"Jesus Christ! Look at all these *meshugganah* people standing out here!"

The voice was familiar. I turned and looked up. Brad Garrett, all six feet, eight inches of him, stood beside the queue. He threw back his shoulders and strode up and down the line, inspecting the tourists. Everyone recognized him from television and films. He was one of the funniest entertainers I knew.

"What's wrong with you people?" he demanded.

The crowd burst out laughing, obviously thrilled that Brad Garrett was berating them. Some applauded.

"Why are you clapping? There's nothing here you should be clapping about! You guys can't be very smart, standing out here in the wind and liking it! I mean, look at you," he added in disgust.

"You're the most *farklempt* group I've ever seen!" He singled out a woman in a slinky gown and brought her to his side, where everyone could see her. "And you—you're shaking!" He continued his outraged inspection. "You all need to do jumping jacks to keep warm. Let's go! One-two! One-two!"

Everyone, myself included, was doing jumping jacks . . . or at least trying to while laughing.

Brad went nose-to-nose with a man having trouble coordinating his legs and arms.

"If you can't do this, Private," he said with a drill sergeant's sneer, "I will get the trampoline out of my car and assist you in the art of jumping."

We were all hysterical. Brad thumped the "private" good-naturedly on the back, then he hugged me, shook a few hands, and disappeared into the hotel.

I needed that laugh. A week had passed since my row with Dick and since Paolo offered his friends' services. Having filed a formal complaint against my supervisor with Human Resources and knowing an investigation would soon be under way, I was trying to keep a lower profile than usual. Something would happen on that front soon.

At home, Cassy and I weren't seeing much of each other. Her outings were like the proverbial dead elephant in the middle of the living room: we both knew it was there, but we were pretending it wasn't, so we wouldn't have to talk about it. The situation was eating me up inside, and as crazy as work was, I preferred standing under the porte cochere to sitting at home.

I turned to the next person in line.

"Hi!" a fresh-faced young woman bubbled. "I'd like to go to the Golden Nugget."

I waved for a cab. When I turned back, the woman's expression had clouded over. "May I ask you a silly question?"

"Sure," I said.

"Do you guys get earthquakes here? I thought I felt the earth move about an hour ago, and I heard a rumbling that frightened me."

"You can relax. That wasn't an earthquake," I told her. "The federal government has resumed nuclear testing out near the air-force base."

She blanched. *"What?"*

I held up a hand. "I'm kidding," I told her quickly. "You felt the vibrations of a moment in history—the implosion of the Aladdin Hotel."

Her brow wrinkled for a moment. "Isn't that where Elvis Presley married Priscilla?"

"Hey, you're good," I said, surprised.

"Ask me anything about Elvis."

I recalled my guidebook research. "What entertainer gave Elvis the idea of wearing a rhinestone-studded jumpsuit?"

"Liberace. Next question?"

"Whoa, I surrender! You're out of my league."

"So how could anyone knock down a building with so much history?" She looked all shook up.

"The Aladdin was too small by today's standards," I answered as Piccolo Pete drove up. "A bigger hotel will be built in its place."

She nodded, and I helped her into Pete's backseat, then leaned in the front passenger window to talk to him. On the seat next to him was his little friend the clarinet. "You know anything about the Aladdin's history?"

"You mean why turning the place into a pile of bricks is a public service?" he asked, smiling. "Yeah."

"I'd really love to hear about it," the young woman said.

"My pleasure," Pete said. He intoned gravely as he wiggled his fingers, "The Mystery of the Aladdin." As he pulled away, his fare leaned forward, listening.

Not many people knew about the Aladdin. The Professor had suggested I look up the hotel's history. I had been fascinated and shared what I learned with Pete. The background of the Aladdin was fraught with dishonesty, bankruptcy, enmity, lost fortunes, audacious robberies in broad daylight, queered deals, lawsuits, changes of ownership, and plain bad luck. Pete's fare would enjoy her ride, hearing about the hotel's past.

At the other end of the general-knowledge spectrum was the federal government's nuclear-bomb test program in the Nevada desert. Everyone had heard about it, but few realized that the atomic bombs exploded aboveground only sixty-five miles from Vegas or that they packed a wallop dwarfing the atomic bombs dropped on Hiroshima and Nagasaki, Japan, during World War II.

Most astonishing to me, though, was the city's willingness to serve as ground zero for a total of 235 bombs over a twelve-year stretch. Vegas residents embraced the news in a manner similar to the Hoover Dam announcement of two decades before— a huge government project to bolster the local economy. Vegas being Vegas, the Chamber of Commerce transformed flash and fallout into a tourist attraction.

The citizens learned about the test program only two weeks before the first A-bomb detonation, so the campaign to market Las Vegas as Atomic City, USA, went into rapid development. The mushroom cloud became a symbol for the city. Showgirls balanced towering headdresses shaped like a mushroom cloud as audiences quaffed new alcoholic concoctions called "atomic cocktails." Buses trundled tourists as close to the test site as the government would allow, where the visitors would enjoy an "atomic box-lunch picnic." Upon returning to the hotel, the visitors crowded the lobby gift shops and purchased nuclear-bomb-shaped candy and other atomic-themed games, postcards, and souvenirs.

Now I turned back to the cab line. At its head was an extremely high-strung group we called *gypsies*. I inhaled deeply and took a head count. Fifteen adults and children. The adults wore a blend of Giorgio Armani and Salvation Army: headdress, beads, muumuus, and sandals. The children were always remarkably well dressed.

T-bone came outside just then, and I caught his eye. He looked at me with sympathy. Whenever we dealt with the gypsies, we encountered problems. Sometimes they couldn't decide where to go. Occasionally they lost track of someone in their group, which brought the cab line to a full stop. It was always something.

Since the Grand's opening, I had become an expert of sorts at dialects, but this group spoke with unparalleled speed in a jumble of what I guessed to be European, South American, and possibly Middle Eastern languages. The members of the group all talked—yelled—simultaneously, and I had trouble latching on to even one comprehensible word.

"Where would you like to go?" I asked.

"New York, New York."

"Excuse me, sir. New York, New York is right across the street." I pointed. "Would you like to walk over there?"

"We very tired. Taxi, please," he responded.

"We will need several cabs to get all of you to your destination."

"No, no, no, we go one car. Please don't give us problem. I tell hotel boss," he threatened.

Suddenly the whole group was screaming insults at me. The guests in the cab line began yelling because of the delay, but the frenzied gypsies ignored them.

I noticed Carmine standing across the driveway, under the palm trees. He seemed baffled—this from a guy who killed people for a living.

"Five people only!" I kept repeating.

A large woman waved a hotel towel over her head for attention. She wore loops of beads around her neck and up and down her arms, and every time she moved, she sounded like a beaded curtain. "Don't worry! Relax!" she shrieked at me.

T-bone appeared at my side. "We need to be patient with this tribe," he cautioned.

"No shit, Sherlock," I responded through locked jaws, and he helped me load the group into three cabs.

As the last vehicle drove away, I noticed the clan had discarded candy wrappers and soda cans on the sidewalk where they once stood. As I scooped up the trash, I came within a couple of inches from the birdlike legs of the next woman in line.

I straightened. She looked to be in her twenties, with lank hair and a bloodless complexion. Her companion was hugely overweight and well into his sixties, with hair dyed jet black. I guessed she was his escort for the evening.

"We'd like to go to the Red House, please," he said.

The Red House was a private home owned by a man who hosted sex parties there every weekend. It was in reality a swingers club, which the police shut down periodically when the neighbors complained and a local election was in the near future. With no laws to prevent consenting adults from pursuing their sexual proclivities in a private residence, the Red House reopened for business almost immediately.

I sneaked another look at the odd couple. He had forty-plus years on her, and they were going to a sex club. I did the math: He'd be dead in two hours. "Have a nice time," I said as they pulled away.

"Hi, where are you off to?" I asked the next bleary-eyed guest. She was in her forties, with coarse skin. Her smeared eye makeup brought Bela Lugosi to mind.

"The MGM, please." Somehow her bass voice didn't surprise me.

"You're already at the MGM. You don't need a cab to stay here," I told her, then murmured, "although a shot of B-12 probably wouldn't hurt." As she clomped away, I looked at, uh, her well-developed calf muscles and big-boned ankles. A man. Definitely.

"Cab!"

I turned to see a businesswoman in a finely tailored suit holding an expensive-looking briefcase. She had walked past me to the curb.

"Cab!" she called again, with her arm raised.

"Excuse me, ma'am. The cab line is right over here."

She eyed me. "I don't care where the line is. Just get me a taxi, please."

"I'm sorry, ma'am, but to be fair, I have to take care of these people who have been waiting in line. If you'll wait your turn, I'll be happy to get you a taxi."

Her gaze flicked to my nametag, and then she strode back into the lobby. In less than a minute she returned with two hotel executives. "This is the man who was rude to me." She pointed at me. "I demand you take appropriate action."

"Rest assured we will take care of the matter," one of them said. I watched as he subtly bowed to her. Meanwhile the other man signaled for a limousine.

I stood silently until her ride took her away.

The executives turned to me. "*She,*" one of them said, "is a major stockholder."

The two men listened patiently to my side of the story.

"I've dealt with her a few times," the other fellow said, and shook his head, making his opinion clear.

"So you won't put a letter in my file? . . ." I asked. The timing could not have been worse. I was sure Bug-eyed Dick was all ready to give Mrs. Levine and the HR investigators an earful.

"I wish we didn't have to," he said. "But just in case she checks on us, we need to cover our ass."

"But—" I was feeling weary. Again.

"It will be a *mild* letter," he assured me, then he and his colleague went back to work.

Eleven-thirty, twelve, twelve-thirty. Pretty soon T-bone would be leaving for home.

"I'm going inside to count, man," I told him.

"I'll handle the door," he said as he dug his tips from his pockets and handed the wad to me.

I went inside and divided the evening's take fifty-fifty.

"Jay!"

I looked up to see one of the baggage girls standing a few feet away.

"T-bone said to come outside."

"Is he okay?"

"Looked fine to me," she said, then made for the elevators.

I shot outside, worried. "What's up?"

He looked very excited. "I just opened a door for Mr. P. Check it out, man!" He held out his hand. A small stack of bills lay in his palm. The top couple were hundreds.

"They all hundreds?" I asked.

He nodded.

"Christ! How much?" My excitement matched his.
"Fourteen hundred." He grinned. "That makes up for a couple of bad weeks."

"Just for opening a door," I asked, "or did you blow him, too?"

Mr. P. was an extremely wealthy and famous man. He flew into town on his own completely equipped, fully staffed jumbo jet—a lavish home in the sky. Management spent millions to entice players like him to their hotel. He was the ultimate "whale"—a hotel term applied to only the biggest players in the world.

While high rollers thought nothing of throwing hundred-dollar bills at staff who opened doors, served drinks, or delivered breakfast, the real big guns raised the word *tip* a whole new meaning. Mr. P.'s history of gambling and tipping made him a legend.

During one of his visits, he played for the casino, which meant he had agreed to play a high-stakes game and give away all winnings as a tip. At the end of the game, he had accumulated $1.5 million, which he left as a thank-you to be divided equally among every dealer in the hotel.

Now Paolo strolled over to join the conversation. "You know Anne Ettinger?"

"Isn't she a cocktail waitress in the Tabù Ultra?" T-bone asked.

Paolo nodded.

"How do *you* know her?" I asked my partner.

"Whatever," Paolo said. "She's a good girl. Anyway, the hotel assigned her to take care of anything Mr. P. needed while he played his game. Anne worked her ass off for him, but when he left town, he didn't tip her." Paolo shook his head. "She cried for days."

"What, he just forgot?" T-bone asked indignantly, and looked down at our stack of bills.

Paolo snorted. "No, he didn't forget. A few days later, Anne's bank sent her an official satisfaction of her mortgage. Mr. P. had paid off her fucking mortgage in full."

"Think he'd mind if I had my credit-card company contact him in advance?" I asked.

"Hey! Look who's here!" T-bone said, and pointed behind me.

I was surprised to see Sam walking toward us. He hung out with us, bullshitting, till the end of my shift, then he took my arm and guided me toward his car while he talked. "I heard you're going through something with Cassy, man."

I groaned. "Maybe I should just rent a marquee on the Strip."

"Hey, come on, man." He sounded hurt. "Ain't I your friend?"

"Of course you are, Sam."

"Then I should know all about this shit."

Like I hadn't wanted to tell him for weeks. But I left that unsaid. He was here now. He led me to a Ford Taurus.

"You get a new car?" I asked.

"Nah. Mine's in the shop. I'll tell you about that later. First I want to hear what's goin' on with you and Cassy."

I settled into the passenger seat, and told him the whole miserable story while he drove. "I warned her she could get into trouble just by letting someone buy her a drink. But you know Cass, denial explodes out of her pores."

"This guy married?"

"Yeah."

"Kids?"

"Yeah."

"You and Cassy talk about it yet?"

"Finally. A little. She says they're just friends. They go to shows and out to dinner while his wife and I are at work. All very harmless."

"You believe that?"

I felt a wave of nausea. "No. She hangs out at the bar at the Palms all the time so they can be together on his breaks."

Sam grunted in disgust. "She move in with this asshole?"

"No. We're still at home. She's upstairs, I'm downstairs. She's out, I'm in." I shook my head. "Not so different from before, I guess."

I finished describing our situation as we parked in front of the Peppermill Casino, a place we used to frequent for dinner and breakfast. I was halfway to the door, telling him about Paolo's offer, when I turned to see a strange-looking object in his hands.

"What's that?" I asked, pointing.

"It's the foam model of my next project. I had it in the trunk."

"I'm glad you're making good use of your time." I eyed the thing—I had no label for it. "It looks like the inside of a grouper's mouth with bad dental hygiene. No offense, of course."

He laughed out loud. "Just open the door for me."

I got a closer look at it after we went inside the lobby. The thing was painted gray and brown and turned out to be a mockup of an underground nightclub, which Sam planned to call The Cave. What I thought were teeth were supposed to represent stalactites and stalagmites. Once I figured it out, it actually looked great.

When we sat down, he detailed his plans and explained the club's layout. His eyes shone, and his gestures were animated.

"I've never seen you so excited about anything. I'm happy for you, man."

A smile lit his face. "Yeah. I feel really passionate about it." He carefully set the model beside him in the booth.

"How will you finance it?"

"You mean on a limo driver's salary with a new baby when my wife isn't working?"

"Something like that." I paused. "I'd help out, but all my money's tied up in the spec house."

"Any prospects?"

"Nah," I said in disgust. "The mayor saw it the other day and liked it, but . . ." I shrugged.

"To buy?"

"To rent. At least that would pay the mortgage."

"And maybe she'd like it enough to buy it."

"Maybe. That'd be great." I sighed, thinking of the financial disaster a divorce would cause. God damn Cassy. What a mess.

"I've got almost fifty grand set aside."

"Jesus, man! Where'd you get that kind of money?" I asked.

"Pyramid. Three times, sixteen grand each time."

Sam always had great luck with those get-rich-quick schemes that depended upon bringing in new members whose "membership dues" went to the person at the apex of the pyramid. The odds of making money were terrible, so every time he asked me to join a group that was forming, I declined. Then I'd end up kicking myself as he raked in the dough.

He talked through dinner about his plans for The Cave, his work with the limo company, and his training goals. He pulled out his wallet and proudly handed me photos of his wife and their tiny daughter. The light was terrible at our table, so I walked the photos into the lobby to get a better look at his family.

"They're beautiful, man," I said when I returned to the table and handed him the pictures. "Both of them. You are one lucky fucker."

"Yeah . . ." he agreed, but he sounded as if all his energy was gone.

We paid the check and strolled outside to the Taurus. Sam suddenly grabbed my arm, stopped me, and said, "Jay, don't do it!"

"What?"

"Don't do anything stupid, man." His voice was firm, level. "About Cassy and her boyfriend."

I shrugged. "But Paolo and Carmine—"

"Don't you got ears? Didn't you hear what I said? You need to get calm!"

"They wouldn't kill him or anything."

Sam snorted. "Jay, you are a good man. You got a fine heart. Much as you think you'd want this motherfucker worked over, if it happens, you'll carry it on your back the rest of your life."

I got into the car and sat in sullen silence while he stashed The Cave model in the trunk and then slid behind the steering wheel.

"Am I right?" he pressed.

We both knew he was right, but the thought of Nick's broken bones comforted me.

"Am I right?" he repeated, shoving my shoulder.

"I'll think about it." That was as much as I was willing to give him.

We drove for a while in silence. I didn't know where we were going, and I didn't much care. I had the next day off, and if Sam had the time, I'd hang with him till I had to go back to work.

"Could you forgive Cassy and let her come back?" he asked.

"No fucking way!" I answered immediately.

"Why not?"

The truth was, as much as I had thought about little except her and Nick, forgiveness had never occurred to me. "She's making a fool of me. I get calls at work—lots of them. 'Jay, I saw your wife with this guy Nick, and they look pretty friendly.' Or 'Jay, this is what's happening. You need to wake up to it.'"

"This ain't about your pride, man. It's about if you love her enough to work on it after your marriage has broke down."

"I don't know," I said, miserable.

He pulled into a parking lot and brought the car to a stop. I looked through the windshield to see where we were. It was the topless dive we'd been to before. I didn't know why Sam would like this place enough to come back, but what the hell.

I opened my door, but Sam stopped me from climbing out. He pointed to the car's interior light, so I closed my door, inviting back the darkness.

"You better come up with an answer, man," he said.

"Why?"

"'Cause as soon as that dude's wife finds out, he is going to dump Cassy." He shifted in his seat to look at me full in the face. "He ain't gonna risk losing his kids."

"Yeah? How can you be so sure?"

"It happened to me." His gaze turned toward the club entrance. "It's happening to me."

"Oh, God, Sam. That dancer? . . ."

He nodded. "Capri. Sheila says I gotta stay away from Capri and promise not to see her again."

"Jesus Christ! Then what the hell are we doing here?"

Sam's face twisted with anguish. "I can't do it, man. I love my wife and my baby, and I've tried so hard for them, but I can't stay away from her."

I had counted on Sam for support, but his problems were even messier than mine. I offered to help him, but I needed to hold on to whatever strength I had left. Besides, I doubted he wanted to be free of Capri's magic. If a professional athlete didn't have the self-discipline to control his destructive side, then who the hell did?

Everyone around me was caught in the current and drowning. I realized with a start that I was, too. Had that desire to self-destruct always been inside me? Was it the magnet that had attracted me to T-bone and Sam and Cassy? Had I unconsciously sought out people and situations that would drag me to the bottom so I could learn who I was and then

save myself? I wasn't sure. I would have to give that more
thought when I wasn't so tired. All I knew was that an aspect of
myself also existed in my wife and my two closest friends. No,
I didn't mean Todd's drug addiction or Sam's affair with a crazy
lady or even Cassy's seeing someone else. I meant living the
death wish and living it large.

CHAPTER FIFTEEN

"Jay, this is Mrs. Levine from the Human Resources office calling. I'd like you to take a few days off from work while the department conducts its investigation."

I stood in the kitchen, smearing peanut butter on whole-wheat toast and feeling grateful her phone call hadn't awakened me. My voice sounded alert and sane. "Thank you, Mrs. Levine, but that won't be necessary. I don't mind coming in and doing my job."

"Your taking time off is mandatory during this part of the process, Jay," she said firmly. "I don't anticipate the investigation will take very long, and as soon as we're ready with our findings, I'll let you know."

"I assume Dick also—"

"Yes. Procedure applies to everyone, no matter what their position."

When the conversation ended, the extent of my relief surprised me. I was emotionally exhausted from everything that was going on in my life and around me. I brought my sandwich and a mug of coffee to the kitchen table when the phone rang again. I took a quick sip and said hello.

"Hey, dude. I have news."

"Hey, T-bone. I was going to call you in a little while. I have to take a few days off—"

"I heard. Listen. I'll keep you up-to-date on whatever facts and rumors come my way."

"Uh, okay." I half wanted to know and half didn't.

"So here's your first news flash. Mrs. Levine called in Reverend Dick's disciples, to hear their side of what happened."

"I don't want to hear this, do I?"

"Probably not," T-bone said. "The boys refused to be witnesses. I heard they were really pissed when she pressured them for answers. So they told her nothing happened." He paused. "That doesn't make sense, does it?"

"It doesn't have to," I said. "It all boils down to one fact. Dick will make sure everything gets turned around so he seems innocent. He believes he can go as far as he needs to with his lies, so long as he asks God for forgiveness on Sunday and feels his sins and his soul are cleansed."

"Whew. That's pretty heavy," T-bone said after a moment. "That makes him worse than Sharkey, doesn't it? I mean, Sharkey doesn't try to hide what an asshole he is."

I thought Todd's remark was pretty perceptive, considering the density of his mental fog. "Yeah. We all know how dangerous Sharkey is. He gets off on scaring us. Dick is more sinister, I think. He comes across as a good guy, but he has his secrets, just like everyone else."

"What do you think he's hiding?" T-bone asked.

"Among other things, that he's a snake. He'll lie very still and quiet, pretending to be your friend while he's pushing his agenda at you."

"Like recruiting you to join his group?"

"Exactly. Then, when he realizes you won't go along with his plans, he'll strike, and his venom can flatten you. But he'll get away with it because no one can believe this clean-living man is capable of this kind of shit—all because he's a liar, plain and simple. Then he receives God's unconditional forgiveness on Sunday, and Monday is a new day."

"Do you think he has an agenda for me?" Todd asked.

"Probably. We'll find out, I'm sure."

"Well, if all that is true, it's too bad Mrs. Levine isn't calling in *your* buddies to back *you* up."

To me, that was a mixed blessing. Although we doormen were isolated from the other departments, I still had plenty of friends on the staff—in Security, in the pit, and, of course, in Transportation. As for my own area of hotel operations, I knew every bellman, valet, baggage handler, front-desk clerk, and doorman. Did I trust any of them enough to speak in my defense? Sadly, no, and that included T-bone and most of the other doormen. With the possible exception of the Professor, they would do almost anything to keep their nose clean. We were scrutinized more closely than most other employees, and we were always on camera.

"This is really a big deal at work," T-bone said happily. "Everyone's really into it."

"Thanks, man," I said. "I'm glad I'm providing a PG-rated show."

"C'mon, Jay! I'm saying it only 'cause it's true. Employees get into shit all the time, but a doorman getting into trouble? This is 'breaking news,'—you know that! We're the elite. We make more money than anyone else on the Strip. Probably hundreds of people are praying for you to get fired, so there'll be a job opening."

I rubbed my eyes. Was he listening to himself? "I gotta get off the phone, man. You're bringing me down."

"Wait, Jay! You don't know the best part! You gotta hear this! It's about Cassy's little after-hours fucker."

"What about him?"

"Well, you know Sean. . . ."

"Yeah." Sean was one of my buddies who worked in Security and loved me for some reason. In the middle of the night he would sometimes walk over to the porte cochere just to shoot the shit with me. He was also a maniac. A natural fighter, he had an explosive temper and a reputation of hurting people.

"Well," T-bone said, "Sean walks into the bar at the Palm, grabs a stool right in front of this Nick the bartender dude, and says, 'Gimme a tequila shot.'"

I was sick to my stomach. "That's great. The guy's got brass balls. Listen, I gotta get off the phone."

"No! Wait!" T-bone shouted. "Sean stares at Nick. I mean stares like he's really angry, using his eyes to burn a hole in the scumbag's face."

Now the story was getting interesting. "Then what happened?"

"Sean knocks back the shot, sets the glass down real hard on the bar, and calls for another. Nick brings it to him, and Sean gulps this one down, too. Then he stands up and—get this!— says to Nick, 'You know Cassy Rankin?' So Nick says, 'Yeah.' So Sean says, 'I'm a friend of her husband's,' and he slams the empty shot glass down so hard on the bar, Nick jumps backwards. Sean glares at him again, like, 'You're lucky this wasn't your head. This time.' And then he walks out of the bar."

"That's great," I said, feeling the coffee roiling in my stomach. "Thanks for calling, dude. I gotta go."

"Wait! One more thing! And that'll be it! I promise!"

"What, already? Jesus!"

"Guess who has a brand new truck?"

"I dunno. Tell me."

"A Dodge Dakota Laramie, with a fucking quad cab and four-wheel drive and leather-trimmed seats?"

"Who, goddamn it?"

"Fucking D-man." T-bone loosed a maniacal, high-pitched laugh. "The hotel tried to hold on to that fucking diamond ring as long as possible, but the Lost and Found finally had to hand it over. A fucking Laramie, man, painted bright—"

"Thanks, T-bone," I said, and let the handset drop from my fingers into the cradle. I sat staring at it. I was too numb to think and too upset to know what to do.

After a few minutes I brought out my stash of drugs, sat on the sofa, and looked at the inventory. I needed a break, a time out from my life. I fingered the various bags and bottles and finally selected a pill. My choice to soothe my turmoil was a painkiller. Funny name for a pill, I thought. Kills the pain and maybe does me in at the same time.

Some drugs lessened the misery by making me feel stronger and bigger than whatever was hurting me; other drugs numbed me to myself. But the painkillers thawed out my brain when it felt like a shit-laced glacier. The pills were like a mental icebreaker, allowing me to coast through my problems as easily as if I were gliding through butter.

I shook two from the bottle and swallowed them dry, then rested my head against the back of the soft, loose pillows of the sofa. For once I didn't feel like turning on music. The house was silent but not peaceful. The quiet had weight and dimension. It felt forlorn, abandoned, bereft of the love it had once known.

I closed my eyes and tried to think about my life. Where it was going? I tried to conjure up an image of the future, but I had come to the end of my game. I had no goals, no good feelings about myself. My life had slowed, stopped, and then moved in reverse. My only hope was that the drug would kick in and keep me alive instead of stopping my heart.

I drifted. I traveled deep inside myself, looking for the cross-roads where I had taken the wrong path. At my core I never wanted to be seriously self-destructive, but with so much of my life broken, I was vulnerable to whatever would tear me down. I had lost touch with who I was, then no longer felt accountable for my actions.

Could I live differently? What would that look like? Could I learn how to be happy? Then maybe things would be okay. Then I could find hope somehow, somewhere. Maybe I would meet a woman capable of loyalty and worthy of respect. I might find a friend who wasn't stuck in his own shit.

Oddly, I began to feel better. Then I remembered; the drug was kicking in.

The phone rang, and the sound jarred me from my thoughts. I decided to let the answering machine pick up. It was T-bone again.

"Dude! I forgot to tell you! Mrs. Levine called Dick in today to answer your formal complaint. You're gonna love this. Dick filed his own formal complaint against you! Everybody's talking about it. He claims you went postal, and—I quote—he fears for his life."

The machine's tape rewound, and within the minute the telephone rang again. I massaged my temples and waited, annoyed, to hear the caller's voice. What the fuck else had Todd forgotten to tell me?

"Jay, this is Mrs. Levine, from the Human Resources office. Please come to my office tomorrow at three. I would like you to reply to complaints brought against you by your supervisor. You're still on administrative leave, so don't plan on returning to work just yet."

Sam was waiting in the Human Resources outer office when I left Mrs. Levine's office. I had told her what happened with Dick. The rest was up to her.

"Hey!" I said. "You here for an appointment?"

"No, I went looking for you, and Todd said you were here. Hungry?"

The apprehension of meeting with Mrs. Levine had taken a lot out of me, and I wasn't hungry. Had the invitation come from anyone else, I would have said no. But with Sam, I always took on the role of listener. I was up to that. "Let's go, man," I told him.

Except for rare occasions, Sam and I would grab a snack in the massive hotel cafeteria, where the decibel level, on a scale of ten, was a constant ten. The sound of hundreds of conversations, laughter, silverware, and glasses, plus twenty blaring television monitors ricocheted off the walls and ceiling. The fluorescent lights contributed a cold starkness to the harsh environment.

In exchange for the convenience and low price of the food, we forfeited ambience. That wasn't an issue, though. But today, as I took the turn toward the cafeteria, I felt Sam's hand on my arm.

"No," he said. "Not there."

I held my questions till we were at his car. The sun was shining, and his Caddy looked like new. "Wow! You got your car back! It looks great!"

"Thanks," he said without his customary enthusiasm.

"Uh, they did a great job."

"Yeah."

We took off down the Strip.

"Peppermill?" I asked.

"Unless you don't want to . . ."

"No, that's fine." I looked at his hands gripping the wheel. "Sam, if you weren't a black dude, I'd say it was white-knuckle time. What's up?"

He blew out a deep breath. "Jay, I had to get the car painted. Capri poured acid on it. Ruined the paint job."

"*What?*"

"Oh, yeah. Because I tried to break up with her. She also slashed my tires. Twice."

I sat incredulous.

"Who would think she'd even give a shit if I broke up with her, you know? A thousand guys are lined up to take my place—all smarter, richer, better looking . . ."

"Single?" I hadn't meant to say that.

"Yeah, single, too. But she tells me she loves me."

We rode in silence. I waited for him to continue talking if he wanted to. Sam was underestimating his value as a person, but this conversation wasn't about that. As well as I knew him, his experiences, successes, and talents continued to amaze and impress me. He was a very special guy who could probably do anything he wanted. He had the gift.

In my opinion, his only hurdle was his difficulty focusing on one idea and going after it. Sam wanted to do twenty things. He couldn't find that one activity to consume and satisfy him. It was as if he needed to be the light-heavyweight champion of kickboxing and the number-one cyclist, while excelling at ten other projects in his spare time.

Besides training to fight again, he was researching possible locations and investors for The Cave. He was trying to be a world-class cyclist, a good father, a good friend, and a reliable limousine driver. He was trying to balance his marriage and his affair. Over our first round of drinks at the Peppermill, he told me about researching a stock currently selling at ten cents but carrying the potential of reaching fifty dollars a share.

In Sam's life, it was all a top priority. Everything occupied the same level of importance. What the fuck was he trying to prove? I wondered. Wasn't it enough to have a happy little family and a good job? He was all over the place. What was he looking for? Himself?

But this was Vegas. Everyone wanted something other than what they had, and everyone wanted to be someone they weren't. The big difference between Sam and most everyone else, though, was that he had the talent to do whatever he turned his mind and energy toward. That fact raised him above us mere mortals, but it was also creating his downfall. It prevented him from soaring while it dragged him straight to hell. But who was I to judge anyone?

He turned the conversation to Cassy and Nick. "Have you called off Paolo and Carmine?" he asked.

"No, I'm still having too much fun thinking about it," I confessed.

"Well, be careful, Jay."

"No, Sam, *you* be careful! Right now I'm just fantasizing. You're the one with slashed tires and a fucked-up girlfriend."

He looked at me, startled, then he wilted. All confidence, all bravado, all enthusiasm disappeared. His whole face drooped. "I kept thinking I could keep the affair under control, that I could handle it. I fell for her hard, but so what? I'd always been able to separate the pieces of my life and stow them in little boxes, away from each other. I believed Capri had nothing to do with my marriage."

"I understand, man," I said quietly.

"I couldn't help myself, Jay! I swear I couldn't!"

"I know, man." I looked beyond Sam, to see other diners turning to stare at him as he wept.

"The problem is, Capri's a loose cannon, unpredictable. I never know what crazy-ass thing she might do. I didn't know she had a reputation for acting crazy."

I flashed on my warning to Cassy, that she might find herself in worse danger than she ever imagined could exist. Stupid little white girl. If she could see Sam . . .

"I'd been lying to my wife about where I was, what I was doing. When Capri started acting nuts, I got scared for my family. I had to confess everything, so Sheila wouldn't be caught off-guard. She had to be ready to protect herself and our baby in case Capri—" He stopped.

The thought of Capri throwing acid at Sam's beautiful wife and baby or going after them with a knife sickened me.

"Let's get out of here," I said. "You go ahead. I'll get the check."

He nodded, and minutes later I found him sitting in the car.

"What are you going to do, man?" I asked him.

"I promised not to see Capri again. But, but, I couldn't stay away!" He looked down. "I don't know, man. She's addicting. The chemistry is unbelievable."

"Jesus Christ, Sam." I couldn't hide my anger and impatience. "Don't you know what you're throwing away? Don't you know how hard it is to find a good woman who loves you? Who's willing to have a family with you? That's worth a hell of a lot more than good chemistry in bed."

"I know, I know. I've been an asshole, but all that's going to stop. Sheila gave me an ultimatum. I have to choose between Capri and Sheila and our baby. So I already went to the police for a restraining order, to keep Capri from coming within a hundred feet of Sheila or our house. The police gave it to me on the strength of her slashing the tires. And probably she had a record of crazy shit, although they wouldn't tell me that."

"You did the right thing, Sam. I know it's hard, but it was smart."

He nodded. "There's only one problem, and that's where I need your help," he said. "I haven't told Capri yet."

"What do you want me to do? I'll support you in any way I can."

"Go with me to tell her."

"Except for that. You've got to do it yourself, man. So what if Capri won't make it easy? You're tough. Keep your focus on Sheila, and it'll go okay. Call me when it's over. I'll take you out for a drink."

CHAPTER SIXTEEN

Sam dropped me off at the employee parking lot. The poor son of a bitch reminded me of Samson, stripped of his power. I didn't believe Sam ever meant to hurt anyone; he was who he was, and nothing I could say would change anything. He had to have it all. I attributed the whole mess to the obvious impact he had on women and his weakness for them—whatever the fuck that meant. And yet, in all the time I had known Sam, he managed to keep the drama at a minimum.

But what other secrets had he withheld from me? In our times of quiet talks, certain of his revelations startled me, smacking of self-destruction and a lack of control I never would have expected. Capri was the latest.

Taking on Sam's shit was the last thing I needed, what with the HR investigation, Todd's deterioration, and the possible financial disaster created by the spec house. When all *that* was behind me, maybe I'd be able to figure out my own fucking marriage.

I pulled into the driveway and dug my thumb into the garage remote. The interior light blinked on, and as the metal door rumbled up its track, I glanced at Cassy's half of the garage, where she parked her car. The door inched up. No tires. No bumper. No license plate. No trunk. Three fucking A.M., and her car wasn't there.

All the years with my wife boiled down to this one split second: The marriage was over. The love I felt for Cassy bled out of me, and an impenetrable shield clamped down around my emptied heart. Even if that prick bartender returned to his wife and kids, I would not want Cassy back. I had zero interest in trying to heal our relationship.

I sat in my car for a long time, not thinking, not feeling. When the overhead light automatically turned off, I sat in the darkness. Finally I stumbled inside the house and sank onto the sofa to wait, knowing she might not even bother to come home at all. Nah, she'd be back, I decided. If Sam knew what he was talking about, Cassy would come home because Nick wouldn't want to stay out all night.

Everyone around me had gone fucking nuts, and I was no oasis of sanity, either. I had spent ten years with Cassy. Ten *years,* and all I could think about was not losing everything to her in a divorce. I couldn't start over. Not now. Not again. Not after she crossed the inviolable line.

A few minutes later her car roared into the garage. I looked at the kitchen door until she blew in like a foul wind, stinking like a whore, her makeup smeared, her hair a mess. She was dressed like no man's wife, in black leather.

"You forgot to close the garage door," she said, unzipping her high-heel boots. Then she looked at me, and the expression on my face must have registered through her alcoholic haze. She froze. "What'sh your problem?" Her tone was defiant.

"We're done, Cassy. It's over." I hauled myself to my feet. My whole body burned and ached. "You can have the bedroom, and

I'll sleep in the guest room. I'll find you an apartment as soon as I can, and then you're out of here."

We didn't say another word. I went into our bathroom for my toothbrush and into the closet to grab some clothes for the next day. I thought about my clothes hanging there. I thought about the thousands of dollars in cash hidden in a shoebox in a dark corner behind a pile of shoes. Cassy didn't even know about it, but I had the bizarre thought that everything was at risk-that while I was at work, she would steal my clothes and the shoebox and leave me with nothing.

I lay down on the unfamiliar bed, and the room smelled unused and dusty. I was a stranger there. Nothing would seem safe until I got Cassy out of the house. I had to think of a strategy to protect myself legally and financially. I had to come up with another plan to give me emotional satisfaction. It would combine retaliation and protection. Sam had talked me into calling off Paolo's thugs, and I wouldn't go back on my word to him. But I burned for revenge. If I didn't get it, that would eat away at me for a long time.

I knew from my friends that Cassy was at the Forum every night, hanging out at the bar while Nick worked his shift. He was probably giving free drinks all night to my drunken wife. I didn't know which pissed me off more: his fucking her, as much as she denied that, or his getting her loaded before he fucked her.

She couldn't hold her liquor. What if she lost control of her car on the way home and someone got hurt or killed? As her husband, I could be held legally responsible for damages. Well, I was done being responsible for Cassy.

I laced my fingers behind my head and smiled at the ceiling as, relieved, I repeated aloud, "I am done being responsible for Cassy."

I gave myself one week to come up with a plan.

"He says you're burned out, Jay. He says he fears for his life."
Mrs. Levine raised her gaze from the folder and looked straight
at me, studying my face.

I sat across from her in her small office in the HR department. The investigation had ended, and she called me in to
discuss the findings. I met her calm, gray eyes and kept my
mouth shut. I had learned I could trust her—she was probably
the only ethical person besides me in the whole damned hotel—
and besides, any defensiveness on my part would only give
credence to Dick's accusations.

"No one would confirm the Sermon on the Bench had taken
place," she continued, and flipped through my folder. "You've
been a good employee, for the most part. I see here you grabbed
hold of a five-year-old who had gotten away from his parents,
just as he dashed out into the street. His mother wrote a letter
saying you saved her son's life."

"I didn't know she'd done that. That was nice of her to take
the time."

"Yes, it was. Most people wouldn't have gone to the trouble
once they were home." Mrs. Levine turned a couple pages of
light-blue stationery creased in thirds from being mailed in an
envelope. "And here's something about an elderly woman who
fell, hit her head, and went into shock. . ." She looked up.

"I wrapped my coat around her and brought her to the hotel
clinic. I made sure she was okay."

Mrs. Levine nodded. "Very nice. She wrote a letter to the
hotel president, commending you." She paused. "Is that incident
related to this disciplinary form from the bell captain, complain-
ing about blood on your uniform?"

"Yes."

She shook her head. "Good grief. We must ask our guests not
to bleed when they fall." She turned a few more pages. "This one

came in just a few days ago. You didn't ask your *mother* to write it, did you?" She smiled at me, to let me know she was trying to lighten the mood.

I smiled. "My mother isn't the conspiracy type."

"I didn't think so. This guest says her eyesight is failing, and she inadvertently gave you a twenty-dollar tip for opening the cab door. You handed it back and asked if she had misread the denomination. She had, and she gave you the one dollar she had intended."

Mrs. Levine closed my folder and clasped her hands atop it. "Not an exemplary employee but a good one. If you're guilty of anything, it's probably caring too much, taking things too personally, and having an emotional nature."

"Sounds about right," I admitted.

"Jay, I have not made a definitive judgment regarding your complaint or Dick's. No one will cooperate or corroborate. It boils down to Dick's word against yours."

Often the superior's word takes precedent over the underling's, and I thought I was about to get fired. I opened my mouth to protest, but Mrs. Levine silenced me with a raised finger.

"In my heart of hearts," she said quietly, "*I* know what happened. I just can't prove it."

A great weight lifted from my back. "Thank you," I said. "I know you're giving me the benefit of the doubt."

"And then some," she agreed. "Don't let me down."

"I won't."

"Now here's what I want you to do." She ticked off her instructions on her fingers. "First, let it go, drop it, forget about it. Second, move on. Don't look back. Third, come back to work and focus on doing your job. Continue to be the helpful, caring doorman you have been since you came to work here."

She looked at me with raised eyebrows. "Do you feel sure you can do that?"

"Yes."

"Good, because I'm not finished. Fourth, don't talk to Dick unless he speaks to you first or unless communicating with him is absolutely necessary. In that event, you must be calm and businesslike. You might consider bringing someone along who can serve as a buffer . . . or a witness if need be. Be subtle about that. I don't want Dick to be on the defensive around you. Fifth and last, if you lose your temper again, Jay, I will have no choice but to let you go. That would be a sad day for this hotel." She leaned forward. "Do you understand?"

"Yes. Thank you."

"Good." She smiled and sat back in her chair. The tension in her face relaxed.

Of course I wanted to hear about Dick's "sentencing," but I knew better than to inquire. Word would get around the hotel sooner or later, probably when things had calmed down enough for someone authorized to access the personnel files to sneak a peek at Mrs. Levine's notes.

I was amazed, then, when she volunteered, "The other party has also been advised to take certain corrective measures. He will face dismissal should he fail to maintain the proper boundaries between this hotel and his place of worship."

Mrs. Levine took my folder and set it aside. "Take another two days off, just to rest. You look tired, and we need you in top form for the upcoming fight."

"Why? Am I on the card?" I joked.

She laughed. "Being in the ring will probably be restful, compared to what you doormen have in store from Tyson's fan base."

I tried not to groan at the thought. "I'd like to say hi to Todd and let him know I still have my job. Would that be appropriate?"

"Of course."

She stood, and I stood, too, and she walked me to the door of her office. "Good luck, Jay," she said. "And be careful."

"Careful?" I asked her. "Of what?"

"Sometimes," she said quietly, "the bad guys stay the bad guys."

I checked my cell-phone messages on my way to the porte cochere. The mayor had called, ready to sign a year-long lease agreement for the spec house. With that good news, the Dick crisis pretty much handled, and a couple more days off to rest, I felt some weight had lifted as I walked along the long corridor from the HR office.

When I came outside, T-bone ran up to greet me. His wild eyes were dilated, and he compulsively licked his lips. I didn't know what drug or drugs he was on, but he was definitely whacked. I was used to his being hyper, but he had reached a new dimension, as if a film of him were being played at fast forward.

"So when're you comin' back to work, man? Or did Levine decide to shit-can your ass, after all, just on general principles? Jesus Christ, it's good to see you! I've missed you, dude. I really have. So you better be back for the Tyson fight. It's in a couple of days. You'll be in uniform by then, right? You gotta be! I can't do that shit with no one else but you, buddy. You know that." He started moving back to his station. "So did you just come from Levine's office? What'd she say? Wanna go out for a drink later? We can go to that vodka bar that's carved outta ice."

"Yeah, that sounds good. Call me when you get off." I turned away to say hi to some of the other guys.

Cowboy's taxi came barreling into the porte cochere and rammed right into T-bone, flipping him onto the fender.

Cowboy jammed on the brakes, and T-bone slammed to the ground. He lay on the pavement, writhing and screaming.

"Todd!" I turned and ran to T-bone as he lay on the pavement in a crumpled heap.

Cowboy stood over us. "Aw, shit . . ." he groaned. "I've put a spoke in the wheel now, ain't I? I'm dreadful sorry, T-bone. Jes' didn't see ya. Can you stand up?"

"I don't think you should move him," I said firmly. "We should call an ambulance."

"No!" T-bone cried. He was expelling his breath in quick gusts, like a woman in hard labor. "I'll be fine! Leave me alone for a couple minutes. Just make sure no one runs me over."

I tried to think. The hotel had a policy. We needed to follow it. Okay. Get the supervisor, fill out an accident form. The supervisor takes T-bone to the medical center—and stays with him until T-bone gets transferred to the hospital and admitted or until the center's physician says he's good to go home.

Who was that night's supervisor? Since I wasn't officially at work, I didn't know. I looked around for my replacement so I could find out, but the only staff I saw were Paolo and a couple of valets. They came over, and I stood and asked my friend.

"D-Man," Paolo answered. "He's on dinner break. But we aren't busy. We'll take over the line, so you can worry about T-bone here."

I squatted. T-bone's face was a pain-twisted death's-head mask, and sweat darkened his hair. "We've got to let the supervisor know."

"No!" he rasped. "Your buddy Dick is on duty. He'll use me to get back at you!"

I tried to think straight, for Todd's sake. Was he right?

"I'll handle it, Jay!" he pleaded. "Let me handle it!"

"You need to follow procedure. Otherwise you could get into a lot of trouble."

"Your friend don't want to go," Cowboy said. "Give him a minute."

I looked at Cowboy in disgust. "Whose ass are you worried about?"

I turned back to Todd. "Listen to me. Your injury might be bad enough for a workman's comp claim. Am I right?"

Todd didn't say anything.

"That means you *have* to report the incident. It's a no-brainer, man." I remained quiet while he chewed it over.

"I don't want Dick to think this is a big deal," he said. "And I'll need help getting to his office."

That made no sense to me, but knowing Todd, I'd pushed him as far as he would go. "Whatever. Give me your hand. Cowboy, help me get Todd to his feet, would you? And be careful as hell with him."

I stayed out of Dick's sight while T-bone gimped across the baggage room to the captains' office and then back to me. His face was white. I wondered if he were going into shock.

"What'd you tell him?" I asked.

"I'm trying not to make a federal case of it. I said I was hit by a car, but I acted like it was very minor. I didn't want to show the pain."

I hadn't made sense of his reasoning when he added, "He wants me to go to Security and fill out an accident report, then to bring it back here for his signature."

"Let's go."

I helped T-bone hobble to Security and waited while he filled out the report, then I half-carried him back to the baggage room. Somehow he shambled by himself toward Dick's office.

"Dick?" I heard Todd call out.

"Not here," piped one of his disciples.

"Where is he?"

"Gone home, I guess. He had to leave early."

Knowing Dick had gone, I walked into the baggage room. The young bellboy gave me a dirty look and made a quick exit.

"I can't believe that asshole didn't wait for you!" I said, angered. "He knew you would need him to sign the form and take you to the clinic!" I looked at Todd, and he was grinning. "Why the fuck are you so happy?"

"This is amazingly lucky, Jay. Don't you see? Now I won't have to get drug tested! If Dick had been with me, I'd have been without a job tomorrow."

I helped T-bone put his arm around my shoulders, and I gripped him around the waist, and then we started back downstairs.

"I told Dick about the incident," he continued, "so I think I can add his name to the supervisor's line and make the report official."

"Tell me you're joking! If you forge his signature—"

"Not forge! That would be stupid. I mean *print*. Just to show he knows what happened. And for now, Cowboy can take me home."

We came outside. "You trust Cowboy can take you home without killing you first?"

"Sure, I can," Cowboy said. "I won't even charge you for the ride. That's the least I can do, with you actin' like a Thoroughbred and all." He strode to his cab, to bring it around.

"What if you have a broken back? You could sue Cowboy's employer. You might need to apply for a medical leave of absence. For your own good—and Mary's—you need to be seen by a doctor at the medical center."

He grimaced. "That's the last thing I need, man. I'm going home."

Cowboy jumped out and opened his back door, and we managed, with Paolo's help, to pick Todd up and lay him on the backseat.

"Take it real slow, Cowboy," I said.

"You betcha."

I stood in the middle of the driveway and watched them drive off.

Walking back to my car, I tried to make peace with Todd's decision. If he had taken the mandatory drug test, the lab would have found evidence of illegal drugs *plus* painkillers in his urine. The odds that the Grand would fire Todd were, as he said, one hundred percent.

Dick's not being available to take him to the medical center was, I suppose, a small miracle, and T-bone had decided to play the odds. Who was I to judge him for that?

In two days, I would be returning to work for the big fight. I knew it was going to be insane. I wondered if Todd would be there at my side.

CHAPTER SEVENTEEN

"Todd! *Todd!*"

I looked around at the war zone that had been my work area before the Tyson-Holyfield hundred-million-dollar rematch. The shock of the insanity just moments before left me in a bleak haze. Son of a bitch! What the fuck just happened?

"*Todd!*" I screamed, searching for my partner. Where the hell was he? I wondered if I should check with the EMTs loading the injured into the long line of ambulances . . . if calling his wife now would be the smart thing. I didn't want to worry Mary needlessly, but if Todd had taken another hit to his spine, his days were over.

My cell phone vibrated in my uniform pocket, and I dug it out. The rotating red ambulance lights made the caller ID impossible to read. I just hoped it wasn't Cassy. I couldn't take a dose of her right now.

"Jay! It's me, T-bone!" the voice said.

I was filled with relief. "Jesus, man, are you okay?"

"Compared to what, asshole?" he asked. "To the people who got trampled, I'd say I'm in pretty good shape. Otherwise . . ."

"Where are you?"

"Home, man. When I realized what was goin' down, I got the fuck outta there in self-defense. Paolo passed me in his car as I was walking to the garage, and he gave me a lift home."

"Oh, man, T-bone, I was worried about you."

"You should've been! That was as bad as anything I saw in the marines. I was calling to find out if you're okay."

"I have no fucking idea. Physically I'm okay, but I have to sort out everything. . . ."

I didn't understand exactly what I was saying. The words had just come out. As soon as I heard them, though, I knew something had changed inside me. Just as one specific moment in our garage at home had signaled the end of my marriage to Cassy, seeing the guests lying facedown in blood on the driveway had severed my love affair with the city.

"But we made good battle pay, huh?" T-bone said. "I've been counting the wad since I got home, and I'm still not done. Can you imagine what we coulda done if the fucking place hadn't exploded?"

I looked down at the bulging pocket where I kept my tips. Todd's estimate was probably correct: we made two weeks' worth of tips in two hours. But that didn't matter anymore because something bad and dark was going on inside me. I was in too much pain, and I was too angry to keep going. I had no peace of mind. I felt myself begin to implode.

As recently as the ride to work a few hours before, I craved the energy of this city. I was addicted to the charge, the rush, and the drama that surrounded me under the porte cochere. Las Vegas had been, for me, pure electricity. The power of Vegas, which for years had bombarded and excited all my senses, now overwhelmed me. All at once I was dying from its side effects.

I could not have been more certain of the crisis if a surgeon had shown me an X-ray of my deteriorating heart, lungs, and brain and pointed out the effect of too many years of fearing management. Of choking down my rage at unpredictable guests, mean drunks, and vindictive bottom feeders. Of being surrounded by drugs, hookers, noise, smoke, and flashing lights. Of feeling helpless in the face of problems at home.

Whatever reasons had caused my meltdown, they had stolen most of my humor, maturity, patience, and peace of mind. To survive, I regressed into a primitive version of the man I used to be. My intellect diminished to something basic and dull. I had lost the capacity to think clearly, strategize, or puzzle out situations. My emotional reactions were rapid and strong, and they lacked nuance and control.

I was so fucking unhappy. With so much loss around me, my world had taken on a dark cast that grew darker each day. I always felt tired, as if I were dragging one weighted foot in front of the other. Five minutes after getting to my workstation, I needed to sit down. My physical and emotional energy had faded so drastically, my body wasn't allowing me to be myself. So this was burn-out.

In recent weeks I had tried to stay in the game. I swallowed one drug to feel better and another to help me sleep. Ironically, I was following the same regimen that had caused T-bone's downfall. I had tried to save him but failed. Now my own life was a mess. Could I save myself, or was it too late?

I decided the only way for me to find out was to leave Vegas. Tomorrow morning I would tell T-bone my intentions, and in the afternoon I'd give notice to Mrs. Levine. Before I headed out, I would take care of Nick and Cassy. And then, maybe, once I was away from this place, I would heal. And if I didn't, well, what the fuck. I no longer cared what lay ahead.

I trudged to the employee parking lot and found my car. I slid behind the wheel, locked the doors, and sat for a few minutes in the quiet. I took long, slow breaths and let my mind wander. Sam would be at Capri's now, or maybe he was already on his way back to Sheila.

What kind of a friend had I been to Sam, watching him come undone as he fucked up his life and deciding not to interfere? What the fuck are friends for, if not for that, huh, Jay, you fuckin' asshole? I hadn't wanted to be like Bug-eyed Dick, who had stuck his uninvited nose in *my* life. Well, if I couldn't see the difference between my love for Sam, and Bug-eyed Dick's self-serving manipulation, then I was one sorry bastard.

I was exhausted, but the events of the evening had me too freaked out to go home. My mind raced, and I obsessed about Cassy and Nick. I had already met with a divorce attorney and rented a small but clean apartment for Cassy. She did not know about it yet. I wanted her out of the house on my schedule, not hers.

I was close to formulating a plan to deal with Nick, but it hadn't come together yet. The solution appeared with a blinding flash. I turned on the car's ceiling light and looked in the backseat. The spiral notebook I used as a workout journal to keep track of my progress at the gym was half sticking out of my gym bag.

I pulled it out with the pencil stuck in the coiled spine and began to write.

To the owner of The Palm Restaurant:

Your bartender Nick is getting my wife drunk every night. The purpose of this letter is to inform you that if she gets

into an accident on her way home, if she causes any property damage or injures herself or anyone else, I will hold
you responsible, and my lawyers will come after you.

Beautiful. I folded the note and stuck it in my pocket. I would
copy it onto formal writing paper when I got home, drive it to
the post office, and send it certified and registered, so I'd
have proof of delivery. I'd also send a copy to my attorney for
his records.

The shit was going to fly far and wide when Nick's boss got
the letter. He'd know that piece of shit was pouring free drinks
for Cassy, and if he didn't fire the son of a bitch, at the very least
he would make sure Cassy never set foot in his place again.

My thoughts turned to T-bone. Would he recover enough to
return to work? I suspected he would apply for workmen's
comp within the week. If he didn't bring up the idea himself,
I would suggest it to him. Why risk being confined to a wheelchair for the rest of his life, when insurance programs were there
to help him?

As for me, I needed to move on, as a lot of other employees
had already done. Most came to Vegas to start a new life, but
when they'd gone home for a vacation and seen how old their
parents looked, they realized they needed to move back. Maybe
that's what I would do if I could sell the spec house—settle down
in California. My folks weren't getting any younger, either.

I turned to the next page in my journal and wrote out my
resignation, with two weeks' notice.

The next day, I felt better, having made the commitment to
resign from the Grand. As I walked through the employee
entrance, I couldn't tell if the hundreds of people surrounding
me were quieter than usual or if the din just wasn't bothering me
so much.

Making it down the long corridor to the Bell department had always been an exercise in navigating through the hundreds of people coming to and going from work. That day, I seemed to glide through them.

D-man suddenly stood before me, stopping me in my tracks. He worked the day shift and was on his way toward the door. "Hey, man," I said. "What's up?"

He had an uncharacteristically grim face. "Haven't you heard?"

I strained to hear his question. "Heard what?"

"Aw, Jay, you haven't heard?" he asked me again.

I looked at my watch, worried I might be late. "Heard what, D-man? Tell me."

"Jay, Sam was killed last night."

"*What?* What did you say?" It was impossible.

"He was shot. Jay, he's gone."

I moved to the wall and braced myself for balance. I could feel my mind going somewhere very dark. *Sam? Gone?*

D-man had followed me. "You all right?"

"No. Tell me what happened." Was it possible I'd never see my friend again? Never hear his voice or feel his slap on my back?

"I'm not sure, man. I just heard it going around the hotel, and I know you two were pals. . . ."

"D-man, do they know who did it?"

"I heard he was trying to break it off with some topless dancer he was seeing on the side, and she killed him. Then she shot herself in the head. That's all I know."

His voice reverberated. I was numb, as if I had venom in my veins.

"I'm sorry to be the one to tell you," I heard D-man say as he disappeared into the masses of people. "He was a good guy. Everyone knew it."

He's gone echoed in my brain. So final, irrevocable. I couldn't make sense of it. I felt as if I were watching myself walk to the Bell department. How could I go to work and stand on concrete for eight hours? My mind was spinning. Pain, sorrow, loss, a bullet, Sheila, the baby.

What could I have done to stop this? What could I have said? Who should I talk to? Who *can* I talk to? Tears poured down my face. I got him hired. He'd be alive if I hadn't done that. He had asked me to go with him, and I'd refused. If I'd gone, would he still be alive, or would we both be dead?

I changed into my uniform, trying to wipe my tears off my vest. Would I get into trouble if my vest is wet? A big piece of my life was gone. I was alone in the locker room, and I let myself sob.

"Fuck you, Vegas!" I yelled. But I knew it wasn't Vegas. It was Sam and the way he played his life. If it hadn't been in Vegas, it would have happened somewhere else.

I splashed my face with cold water and then tried to gather myself as I walked toward the porte cochere.

"Jay?"

I turned to see Mrs. Levine coming from the direction of her office. As usual, she had a handful of personnel file folders clutched to her chest.

"Hi," I said. I had to hold myself together.

"I don't want to make you late for work, but I'd like a few moments to chat. Mind if I walk with you?"

"No, I don't mind." Had she heard about Sam, or had Dick accused me of something?

"Have you seen or spoken with your friend Todd recently?"

"Uh, not for a few days. He's been calling in sick—"

"Yes. And he has submitted a claim to workers' comp insurance for permanent disability income. It's based on an accident that allegedly occurred on hotel property."

"'Allegedly'?" I stopped.

"I'm trying to reconcile some discrepancies on the forms and so on." She shooed me to keep walking. "I wanted you to know what is going on, since you and Todd worked together for so long and because someone might be in touch with you from the hotel's Legal department."

"All right. You know I happened to be—"

"Before you offer any answers, Jay, I think you best know the questions." She flashed me a smile that seemed too uncomfortable for our conversation.

"I'm listening."

"First, Todd's supervisor says Todd never reported that he had been—" she looked down at her notes "—struck by a taxicab, to his knowledge."

Mrs. Levine and I both had learned Dick was a liar, plain and simple, especially if it meant saving himself, so I didn't bother interrupting her. He was a fucking poster child for lies and deception.

"He said that if Todd had come in to report such an incident, then policy would have sent both of them to the medical center."

I had a sinking feeling in the pit of my gut.

"The medical center has no records of Dick bringing Todd in, and apparently none of the staff examined the victim of a car accident, ordered X-rays, or admitted anyone to the hospital.

"Although the Security department sent an accident form into processing, Dick's signature is nowhere on the form. Someone printed Dick's name, however, and our Legal department believes that whoever forged Dick's name may be guilty of insurance fraud."

Oh, Jesus. "Mrs. Levine, a very simple explanation for that—"

"I'm not quite finished, Jay. Please indulge me. I won't be long." She turned to her notes. "*Somehow* your friend has found an attorney to represent him in suing the hotel as well as the cab company that employs the driver who allegedly struck Todd."

Emphasis on *somehow*, I noticed. The hotels had created many obstacles for anyone wanting to sue them. First, most attorneys hated going up against the hotels and would refuse to take on a case such as Todd's. Second, all the corporate titans had a battery of top lawyers, and third, the hotels wielded enormous political and judicial clout.

"The cab company's attorney wrote us a letter stating the driver did not file an accident report and denies the incident occurred. The Las Vegas Police Department has no documentation, either. They have asked us to provide a copy of our Security department's videotapes, to clarify what—if anything—actually happened."

"Jesus Christ." Todd would have saved everyone a lot of time and trouble by going to the medical center on the night of the accident and failing the drug test, I thought as we walked through the lobby.

"Did you say something, Jay?" Mrs. Levine asked.

"I don't think so."

I stepped aside as she went through the door to the porte cochere, then followed, looking up at the various lenses pointing at us. With so many security cameras everywhere, Todd's claim would be verified and approved quickly . . . except for one thing that was common knowledge: Security would do anything to protect the hotel from legal problems, and that included deleting film that could be used as evidence.

"So what did the videotapes show?" I asked weakly. The level of integrity of the hotel management was similar to that of Washington politicians.

"They showed nothing." She shrugged and shook her head. "Todd submitted a huge stack of medical bills to the Grand's insurance carrier when he applied for disability status and income. Obviously the hotel's insurance cannot reimburse him until we get to the bottom of this mess."

"So what are you going to do?"

"My only choice is to lay him off pending an investigation of possible fraud." She looked at me hard. "My advice is that you stay clear of this mess. Otherwise you could get into a lot of trouble."

"Mrs. Levine, are you threatening me?" I asked.

"Don't be ridiculous," she said impatiently. "*If* you witnessed something here, you could be considered a coconspirator in an insurance-fraud case and go to jail. And *if* you witnessed something, you can't even be sure what it was. I've seen your friend's medical bills—the number of different doctors he's seen, the classification of drugs he takes. An addict will do anything to get his fix, including stage a car accident, including let his friends take the rap for something he himself did."

I felt a jolt, remembering how T-bone refused to clear my name with Sharkey.

"Everyone involved in this is ready to play hardball, Jay. You don't play in that league. You don't know how. You wouldn't be able to protect yourself, even if you saw danger coming, which I doubt you would. You could get into terrible trouble with the Grand just for being on the property that night. You were not supposed to be here. You were on administrative leave."

"But after our meeting that day, you gave me permission to say hello to Todd, remember?"

She looked straight at me. "No, Jay, I don't. In fact, that never happened."

CHAPTER EIGHTEEN

When was the last time I had worn a necktie? I couldn't remember that or the last time I had been to a funeral. My sadness was so great, I was pretty close to turning my Windsor knot into a hangman's noose. I'd lost too much to handle—my wife, my home, my best friend, and maybe myself.

I sank down on the edge of the mattress, and my heel bumped the small, locked metal box I'd stuck under the guestroom bed. Ten thousand dollars in one-hundred-dollar bills. The secret stash I'd retrieved from the closet floor in the master bedroom. The money used to mean so much—seed money for my new life. Now it seemed worthless because the thought of starting over sucked dry whatever strength I had. Would I ever recover from my bone-deep exhaustion?

I wanted nothing more than to crawl between the sheets and stay there for the week, the month, the year. Overriding that need—the only thing that *could* override it—was the wish to honor my friend Sam.

I heard the garage door rattle up its track. I took a deep breath. Cassy and I hadn't communicated for a week, and we had plenty to talk about. I had received proof of delivery for my letter to Nick's boss, but Cassy had yet to mention anything to me about that or Sam's murder. Maybe she hadn't heard about—?

The kitchen door banged open, and Cassy's footsteps pounded across the floor.

"Who the fuck do you think you are?" she screamed, and stopped in the doorway of the guest bedroom.

I looked up at her. My weariness deepened. "Hello, Cassy."

"Nick's boss put him on probation, and I'm barred from The Palm."

"Cassy"—I hardly had the energy to talk—"I want you to move out of here."

"Gladly!"

"I'm setting you up in an apartment. I found you a nice place." I heard her gasp as I turned and pointed to the dresser. "The key is there, with the address."

"I can't believe you had the fucking nerve to—"

"Let's not talk, let's act," I said. "Just hire a mover. When you've got your half out, leave the house key on the kitchen counter."

As I walked slowly into the Baptist church sanctuary, I felt oddly removed, out of my body, light years away, watching the tragedy unfold. Ten choir members in royal-blue robes took their position on the broad, carpeted steps leading to the stage. Swaying to the organ music accompaniment, they belted out a gospel hymn. Their voices were as strong and deep as my grief. I looked for Sam's wife—his widow—and found Sheila on the stage with the rest of his immediate family. She hugged their tiny daughter to her shoulder.

The sight of my friend lying in the open casket jolted me to a stop, and tears sprang to my eyes.

He hadn't known he was playing with fire. He had no idea Capri was capable of murder. And she, so young and beautiful and seductive, couldn't have thought, *I'm going to move to Vegas and ruin my life.* A few minutes after she murdered Sam, she turned the gun on herself and committed suicide.

I took in a ragged breath. An usher came toward me, and I was grateful for his steadying hand on my elbow as I went to the stage to pay my respects.

I touched Sheila's shoulder, then knelt before her. "I'm so sorry," I rasped.

She nodded, dry eyed. So beautiful. So angry. She studied me, searching. I opened myself and, having nothing to hide, hoped she would find the answers and comfort she sought. After long seconds her lips moved but made no sound, and her eyes brimmed with tears. I left the stage and found a seat in a pew toward the back of the room.

The minister took the podium and nodded at the organist to begin. I had never been to a Baptist funeral. I closed my eyes and concentrated on holding myself together.

The hymn ended, and as the eulogy began, I tortured myself again, as I had since D-man had stopped me in the hall. I had to be partially responsible for this. Again I tormented myself. Sam would still be alive if I hadn't helped him get the job at the hotel. I should have gone to Capri's apartment with him! No, she would've killed me, too, probably. I should have told him that going over there was a lousy idea. He'd be alive if I hadn't . . .

I told myself to shut the fuck up before guilt sent me running for the door.

"Brothers and Sisters," the minister's voice rang out, "do not ask me why. I surely do not know why God took this young man from his family and friends. The reasons do exist. Yes, indeed, in the mind of God is the perfect explanation. If God would but share his secrets, we could make peace with Sam's passing right here and right now and release our sorrow!"

He spread his arms wide. "Now you may *think* you know what happened, but you don't. Ohhh, no, you do not, and I'll tell you why: because your speculation is from a mortal's perspective, and we mortals have limitations. We cannot see everything! We cannot hear everything! We cannot know everything!"

"Amen!" a woman sang out.

"Your best guess in your finest hour here on earth cannot come close to revealing God's mysteries or infinite wisdom."

I had expected a subdued service filled with quiet sadness. I could not have been more wrong or less prepared for what happened next. One by one Sam's family and friends took the podium to let loose their emotions about Sam's murder. Holding nothing back, the mourners unleashed piercing sobs to purge their anguish. Never had I witnessed anything more gut-wrenching. I could no longer hold myself together.

Everyone in the church wept and wailed inconsolably while the ushers walked up and down the aisles, never pausing, to hand out tissues. Some mourners became so overcome by grief, the ushers had to help them from the sanctuary. The hysteria was so awful, the sadness so intense, I couldn't stand anymore. My head spun, and my heart felt torn apart. I stood to leave.

Then I saw Stevie Wonder enter the room. Several people escorted him onto the stage, and the room became quiet.

In shock, I sank back down into my seat. "Oh, Sam," I whispered, burying my face in my hands, "I am so sorry, man. I'm sorry I didn't believe you."

Stevie Wonder spoke with compassion and respect about the profound effect Sam had had on his life. As he described their friendship, he touched on Sam's optimism, his sincere willingness to help his friends, his intelligence, and his astonishing range of talents and passions. He described Sam's endless stream of ideas and his infectious enthusiasm.

Sam had been a friend to a world-renowned musician in exactly the same ways he had touched my own life, and Stevie Wonder had loved Sam for the identical reasons I had.

"Of all my friends," he told us, "I was certain Sam would be the one to succeed."

I had believed that, too. But now he lay in a coffin by the songwriter's feet. Would I ever believe it? Could I learn to accept Sam's death? Would the horrible stabbing pain in my chest ever leave me? The bullet that killed Sam seemed to have ripped a hole in me, too. When he died, a part of me died as well. It lay tucked beside him in the coffin forever.

Stevie Wonder began to sing a gospel song that was intense and powerful. I gazed out over the entire congregation in the rows before me. They all sat head bowed, shoulders hunched, and back rounded, and sobbed convulsively.

I thought I would have had the pleasure of watching Sam focus his energy on one endeavor and make it happen big-time for Sheila, their baby, and himself. And now? What kind of future awaited those whom Sam had left behind? An inner voice whispered, *Can't you remember? You already know.* My throat constricted as feelings of abandonment, loneliness, and deprivation surfaced from my own childhood. I wrapped my arms around my middle and cried my heart out.

"So what have you been up to, man?" I asked T-bone. I'd called him on my cell phone on the way to work.

"Not much. Watching the boob tube," he told me. "Jesus! That reminds me! Have you heard about Oprah's guest this afternoon? What a fucking asshole!"

"No. Who was it?"

"The doorman over at the Hilton," he said.

"He was on *Oprah* today? That's pretty cool." The guy was famous, with moves so amazing, crowds gathered every night to watch his routine. "Why's he an asshole?"

"Because Oprah says to him, 'So how much money do you make?' and without thinking, he answers, 'Three hundred grand a year.'"

"Aw, crap!" T-bone was right; the guy hadn't been thinking. No one declared his true income in tips. Most of us said we made twelve bucks an hour.

"Half the doormen on the Strip will want to shred that guy's ass," he continued. "And I'll bet the Internal Revenue spotters are already thundering down here."

"Yeah, assuming that the norm is some guy at the Hilton who's a performer—"

"—and now a television celebrity—"

"—rather than a regular doorman," I said. "That would be grossly unfair. Besides, players who stay at the Hilton have the reputation of being generous tippers."

"Just think of those poor sons of bitches working at Circus! Circus!," Todd said. "The guests there are supposed to be terrible tippers. I mean, those doormen might be really making only six bucks an hour!"

"I guess I'm leaving at a good time," I said, "between your being out of commission and the IRS standing on full alert."

Silence. I had not told Todd about my conversation with Mrs. Levine. I was hoping he'd bring up the subject.

"Have you seen Cowboy around?" he said at last.

"No, not lately." I pulled into the employees' garage behind the hotel and quickly found a space for my Lincoln—a miracle.

"Tell him to call me when you do." His voice was full of anger, and he spat out his words. "Listen to this, dude. It's so fucking unbelievable. The lawyer for Cowboy's employer wants me to come to her office for a deposition—you know, tell her what happened, while I'm under oath—because Cowboy can't fucking re-*mem*-ber any accident."

"What?" So the fuck was still trying to cover his ass because nobody saw the accident happen.

"And on the very same day she calls to schedule the appointment for a deposition," T-bone went on, "the mailman delivers a letter from her office. Cowboy's boss is offering me two thousand bucks if I sign off from making any future claims against Cowboy and the cab company."

"That might be a good idea, man," I told him. "You and Mary have some money set aside, don't you? And Mary's paid well at her job, right? You could drop the whole thing against Cowboy and his boss. Ask the Grand for a medical leave of absence and use the time to rest up. Take a couple, three months to follow your doctors' orders, get off the drugs and—"

"What are you saying, dude?" Todd asked. "Let it all go? Pretend my back is no worse than a bad cold? I'm falling apart here! My pain is so bad, I can't fuckin' sleep. My three-year-old weighs thirty-four pounds, and I can't pick her up because my back—"

"Todd, I didn't mean you should pretend anything! I'm worried, that's all."

"About what?"

I glanced at my watch. "Listen. I need to talk to you about this, but I have to clock in and get to our station." I started out for the staff entrance.

"Jay, I've seen different doctors, but none has any hope surgery can help me. Most attorneys won't even take my phone call when they hear what my case is about. I'm taking a shitload of painkillers, so I'm on a roller-coaster. Either I'm in agony or I'm so fucked up, I can barely stay awake. I—"

"I know, man. I know." I stopped short of the door. "I can't talk anymore, Todd. I have to go inside. I'll call you later, though. Okay?"

"Of course it's okay, you moron," he shot back. "Where the fuck do you think I'm gonna go? Out dancing or to the fucking gym?"

I ended the connection before I got into the locker room. I did not want Bug-eyed Dick or one of his buddies to overhear me talking with T-bone.

The Professor, sitting on the bench by our bank of lockers, looked up from tying his shoelaces. "I understand you're leaving us," he said. "I'll be very sorry to say goodbye."

"Thanks. And I'll miss your little historical stories on Vegas. I found them interesting." I opened my locker and took out my safari shirt.

He raised an eyebrow. "I hope my stories were instructive as well," he said. "Particularly the one about the mobster and the architect. Do you recall—?"

"Aw, shit! A pop quiz?" I groaned, and the Professor laughed. "Sure, I do. Bugsy Siegel and William Moore. Bugsy had his thugs spill acid on the carpeting of Moore's Frontier resort, but Moore stood up to Siegel."

The Professor smiled. "You have earned yourself an *A*." He lowered his voice. "You, Mr. Rankin, stood up to a bully during your tenure here, and I much admire your bravery."

"Thank you. Really. That means a lot to me," I said, and changed into my explorer shorts.

When the Professor stood to tuck his shirttails into his chinos, his eyes slewed to my left shoulder. "Have you always had that tattoo?"

"No. Got it last night." I looked down at the yin and yang symbol. I felt happy about it.

"Interesting. Most of my students tell me they get tattooed when they are so drunk, a friend talks them into it and then drives them to the parlor."

"I made the decision while sober and home alone."

He didn't need to know the house was so empty, it echoed. Cassy was gone. She had left me the guestroom furniture, the stereo system and albums, one living-room chair, and a metal box holding ten thousand dollars, which she had not found. Indentations in the carpet evidenced where the furniture had been.

I knew Cassy's ways; she would nest. Nick would dump her—if he hadn't already—and she would feel remorseful about her infidelity. She would wonder when would be the best time to talk to me about reconciling. But she was already too late. I had consulted a lawyer and filed for divorce, making sure my ass was protected.

"So," the Professor said, "you had a purpose for the tattoo beyond its decorative function?"

"Yeah, I did. It reminds me to try to stay in balance with my life."

"Admirable," he said, buckling his belt. "I applaud your intentions. Are you a Buddhist?"

"No, I'm not." I finished pulling up my knee socks and attached the tassels. Whatever occupation I might consider in my new life, it would not require tassels or a fucking safari hat.

I put on my shoes and stood, then closed my locker. I looked toward the door.

"I'll walk out front with you," the Professor offered.

"Jay!"

We turned to see Bug-eyed Dick coming toward us as we walked through the baggage room. Remembering Mrs. Levine's advice not to be alone with Dick, I was grateful for the Professor's presence.

"Jay, I know this is supposed to be your last week, but I'm wondering if you would consider staying on for a while longer? You may know Todd won't be coming back, and I had to let Marty go this morning. That leaves us somewhat—"

"You mean the Weasel?" I asked. "Why'd he get fired?"

Dick cleared his throat. "We caught him scalping show tickets to our guests."

The Professor and I exchanged amused glances.

"Thanks for the offer," I said, "but I have to go."

Dick looked at me, startled. "What?"

"Thursday is my last shift."

"But it would be only for a few days," Dick begged. "We have plenty of applicants, so many, in fact, I hardly have time to review all the résumés. But to make sure I—"

"Dick, my answer's unchanged. Thanks for asking, but quite frankly, I'm done here."

My supervisor's face turned pink. "Will you be going to another hotel? If you don't mind my asking?"

"No. My hotel days are behind me."

Dick chuckled. "Oh, come on, Jay. Was it really that awful for you?"

I wanted to push his teeth down his throat. "Dick, let me put it this way: Do you remember a football player named Too Tall Jones? He played defense for the Cowboys."

"Football has never been my—"

"Jones quit football after four years to focus on professional boxing. He was undefeated after six heavyweight bouts, but he left boxing to return to football. Do you know why?" I looked hard at Dick.

He thought for a moment. "I have no idea."

"The reason he quit boxing was—and I quote—'I've never met so many lousy people in my life.' That's why I'm leaving this hotel, Dick, and why I won't give you one more minute of my life. Some lousy people around here think they can lie and cheat all week long, then ask God for forgiveness on Sunday, so they can start the whole cycle again. I don't want people like that around me. They remind me too much of a poisonous snake."

"Bravo!" the Professor said as soon as we were out of the baggage room. We had left Bug-eyed Dick shaking with rage.

"I didn't mean to tell him off," I admitted as we went down the stairs. "He needed to hear it, and I needed to say it. Otherwise it was sort of spontaneous."

"You did well, Jay. Speaking your truth was probably good for you."

I held the stairwell door open, then followed the Professor into the long corridor leading to the lobby. "Can I tell you something I find amazing?"

"I wish you would."

"From the very long list of people I've met in Vegas, you are one of the very few who has neither stabbed me in the back nor turned their life into a pile of shit."

We passed under the lobby's bright lights, and I saw the Professor's face redden. "I feel sad but honored, Jay, that you believe I have earned that distinction."

We went out to the porte cochere. "Well, here we are at last." The Professor held out his hand, and I grasped it. "I wish you all the best in everything you do, my friend."

"Thank you. You, too."

"May I offer one bit of unsolicited advice? . . ."

"Sure."

"Then I will share with you a saying popular in the Far East."

"Let's hear it, Professor."

"'When the elephants dance, the mice get trampled.'"

I waited.

"Please use it as a mantra when tempted to involve yourself in Todd's travails."

"Meaning?"

"Your friend has taken on some powerful and dangerous opponents. I don't think he realizes what he has done to himself or how catastrophic his actions could prove to anyone trying to help him. Someone is going to get trampled—"

"—and it won't be an elephant."

"Precisely."

"I'll keep that in mind. Thanks."

The Professor was about to thump me on the shoulder in friendship, but I stepped back. "New tattoo," I reminded him.

We shook hands again, warmly. I expected him to make for the employees' garage, but he stood rooted to the spot, looking over my shoulder. I turned to see Angel sashaying in our direction. She wore a halter-top evening gown in royal-blue silk, embroidered around the neck. The skirt's long side slit revealed high-heeled sandals of silver leather, with laces that crisscrossed up Angel's shapely legs. She stopped beside me and gave us a seductive smile.

"Professor," I said, "allow me to present the surpassingly beautiful—"

"My two favorite men," Angel said.

"You put Helen of Troy to shame," the Professor told her.

I looked at Angel, then at the Professor, and back again. They seemed to have more than a passing acquaintance.

He cleared his throat. "Well. I must be off. Jay. Angel. Adieu."

I watched as his long strides ate up the distance, then I turned to Angel. "I guess everyone has secrets."

"Of course," she said. "Not to mention needs and desires." She cocked her head and looked at me closely, her eyes sparkling with humor. "Don't tell me you're actually surprised that the Professor—"

"Don't be silly," I bristled, not wanting to hear what she was about to say. I'd had too many surprises in this town already. "I just never had any idea that the two of you might, well, you know . . ."

I knew my reply was lame, but Angel seemed to accept it, so I kept my dignity.

Hookers rarely became friends with hotel staffers; we were all too busy working and trying to make money, so a prostitute would flirt with an employee only if she thought he had potential as a customer. (The only person I'd seen consistently teased by the hookers was T-bone, who was ready for sex with anyone, anywhere, at any time. His single-minded pursuit of quickies was just one more of his addictions.)

I could hardly compare T-bone to the Professor. The latter was, in my opinion, an extraordinary guy, and I wouldn't be surprised if a hooker with a brain sought him out for a few minutes' conversation, to gather fresh material for her small-talk inventory.

I could imagine Angel doing just that. Call girls of her caliber spent time with sophisticated men who would not be interested in the typical street-hooker type. From what little I had seen, Angel would deliver everything expected of a top-rate hooker: Her manners and her conversation were classy, and she always seemed to say the right thing . . . which was the case with me, right now.

"Your getting out of this place is probably a good idea, Jay. You look really burned out."

"I hope I'm doing the right thing," I said. "I don't know if I have the answers anymore."

"Then I'd better ask you a very simple question." Again she studied my face, as if trying to learn more than I was willing to tell her. "What are you doing this weekend?"

Why would she want to know? I hesitated. "Nothing," I replied. "I'm taking my life moment by moment these days."

"Good. Don't make any plans."

"Why not?"

"How about if I cook you dinner at my place, then we spend the night together? No charge, Jay. A freebie."

"Are you serious?"

I felt disoriented standing before her. Many times I had fantasized about Angel inviting me for a free fuck because she found me irresistible. But how often did sexual fantasies become reality?

At that moment just *thinking* about spending a night with her required more strength than I had, but it also felt good to me. Then I wondered if she was kidding.

She understood my hesitation. "I mean it, Jay, yes. You need TLC. That's obvious. It's written all over you. Are you willing to trust that I know what you need and how to give it to you? And can you believe that I never talk to anyone about my clients so our time together will be between you and me?"

"I'm not sure. I'll need to think about it. Okay, I've thought about it. Yes, I would like that. Thank you."

"Would you mind if I just watch you instead of helping out?" I had parked myself on a barstool at Angel's granite breakfast bar and was content to stay put as she prepared our meal by candlelight.

"Not at all." She turned and smiled at me. "This is your night to relax and receive, not to pitch in."

"That's about all I'm capable of doing right now." I knew how to cook, but if she handed me a paring knife and a raw carrot, I probably would accidentally sever an artery. I rubbed my eyes with the heel of my hands.

"Are you all right?"

"Just tired," I said, feeling as if I'd been sucked clean of blood, marrow, and brain matter.

I should have asked Angel for a rain check.

I wanted to memorize every detail of our night, so I could call it up at will and relive it vividly for the rest of my days. Under ordinary circumstances, it would rank as one of the most memorable nights of my life. I yawned.

"Are you all right?" she asked again.

I looked up. Angel stood across the counter and poured me a glass of red wine from the first of three bottles I had brought as a present. She bent forward to rest her forearms on the counter, and the scoop neckline of her peach cashmere sweater hung loose, exposing her breasts.

"I'm a long way from feeling all right," I answered. "I've gone through stuff I never want to face again. I'm pretty raw. I have nothing left to give. I'm sorry. If you'd like me to go home . . ."

She came around the counter to stand beside me. Her fragrance surrounded me. "Don't be sorry," she whispered. Her fingertips touched the back of my neck, and I shivered as she massaged my neck and scalp.

"Feel good?" she asked.

"Are you kidding?" I closed my eyes and gave myself over to the feeling of a woman touching me like this. I realized it had been a long time, too long. "It's wonderful."

"Good. I want you to let go, Jay. Do you think you can do that?"

"I'll try."

"That's all I ask. Let's spend some time relaxing and have dinner later. All right? You seem more tired than hungry."

"Yeah."

She took my hand and led me toward the bedroom. Was I walking in my sleep? I'm not sure. I do know I was following a dream. Angel guided me through the bedroom and into a large candlelit bathroom. In the corner was a sunken bathtub with water jets. She undressed me, undressed herself, joined me in the water, and bathed me. Then she led me to her bed. I floated behind her. I had let go.

Angel massaged my body, and I felt as if God was giving me a much needed break. I knew I was safe with her. She would accept anything I might say or do without judging me for it.

We lay on her bed, and my head rested on her stomach. We talked quietly about life, Vegas, hopes, and plans.

"This sounds crazy, but in spite of all that's happened with my wife and Sam and T-Bone, and all the bullshit I've been through with the hotel, I'm still going to miss Vegas."

"I know, Jay."

"The more people I say goodbye to, the emptier I feel."

"I know."

Angel was exceptionally skilled in every way. I was surprised by her sensitivity and vulnerability and impressed by her perceptions and wisdom.

As desperately as I needed her calm company and gentle touch, I had no expectations that our time together would evolve into something deep or meaningful. This night would not restore my physical strength or emotional health, and it would not allow me to sort out the past or plan my future. As perfect as the evening was, I remained aware that I was a broken man and Angel was a prostitute.

And I was certain I would miss her.

For weeks I had dreamed of chucking my gear into the backseat of the Lincoln and heading toward California, but instead of leaving immediately, I spent uncounted days in the solitude of my home, resting, listening to music, and trying to find myself again.

These days were very dark. I could not give words to what I felt or, more accurately, how anesthetized I was.

I looked forward to the night, just as I always had with Cassy, except now I was alone. I had no desire to be with other people. The idea of going out for a drink seemed like too much work. The only nighttime activity that attracted me was sleep. I couldn't wait to go to sleep. Sometimes I took a pill to help me float into bed. Sleep had always been my escape and a way of recharging. Every night I showered, climbed into bed, and sighed with relief that I had hours and hours of sleep awaiting me.

Eventually I brought myself around to a normal-person's schedule. I had to search for tiny changes in my state of mind. Sometimes, for just a moment, the pain in my chest lifted. Occasionally I would awaken naturally from a dream, rather than bolt upright in bed, covered in sweat, because of night terrors and vivid hallucinations about Sam and Capri.

I needed to resolve my guilt about Sam . . . if only I could access it inside my head. A lot of terrible things had happened to me, but I was wasting my life away by brooding. Sam wouldn't have wanted that for me. I had to give myself a break and begin to let go of my pain.

I signed my name on the last page of the stack of documents, then handed the ballpoint pen across the conference table to my attorney. "Christ. I have writer's cramp," I told him.

"This is how it is, Jay. We're covering all our bases," Jerome said, polishing his reading glasses.

"Don't remind me," I groaned. "I'm almost afraid to see your bill."

"If it'll make you feel better, you can keep the pen."

My eyes burned from the fluorescent lights over the table, but I'd be able to leave soon. Jerome's efficient assistant was signing the various forms now as our witness. The first was the marriage dissolution, which Cassy had already initialed and signed at her attorney's office. A judge would make it official, and that would be that, at least in concept. Cassy was still very connected to me emotionally.

Jerome turned to the completed purchase agreement for my spec house and applied his notary stamp.

"You do okay on this deal?"

"So-so. I made a little more money than I had put into the house."

"In this market, you can be grateful. I know a lot of people carrying double mortgages."

"We're almost done, Jay." He turned the pages of my deposition testimony. The first hearing for T-bone's insurance claim was quickly approaching, and Jerome slowly read over the clarifications I had added in the margins. I was told to keep out of it, but that wasn't who I was.

"Todd's claim can't get settled soon enough for me," I said. "He and his wife are coming undone from the stress."

"That's exactly what the insurers and the hotel hope will happen. They may put off the court date and try to find more witnesses, or they may interview everyone again, hoping for discrepancies between versions. Basically it's just a delaying tactic. If enough time goes by, someone will get desperate enough to settle out of court."

I knew just who it would be, too—the mice, not the elephants.

"So you're really gonna do it, you son of a bitch."

"Yeah, the car's all packed, man, and I'm good to go." I sat down in an armchair near the sofa where T-bone lay and watched television. His house was a mess, especially within four feet of where Todd had settled himself. Littering the coffee table directly in front of him were empty beer cans, a plastic plate with drying remnants of some meal, and amber prescription bottles.

My anxiety flared, just looking at the pigsty.

"I'm glad you stopped in to say goodbye." Todd's eyelids were at half-mast, and he continued to stare at the television even while talking to me. "I'd've been pissed if you called from the road to say adios."

"No way I would've done that, man," I said, although the thought had entered my mind.

He opened a small plastic bag and tapped some of the powdery contents onto the coffee table, and with a tightly rolled dollar bill, he vacuumed all of it into his nose.

I shifted in the chair. After only about three minutes with T-bone, I was desperate to leave. The living room air felt close and still, like in an undisturbed tomb. I could hear Mary upstairs, screaming at their daughter. The kid's cries were high and shrill.

"Fuckin' Mary," he said in a loud, angry voice. "She's so hyper, I can't stand to be with her, and the kid's always jacked up because Mary is."

This is the last thing I need right now, I told myself, and wiped away the sweat from my forehead and upper lip.

I remembered the night Todd had introduced his wife to Cassy and me. Mary was sophisticated and pretty, a multilingual hotel concierge who made very good money.

"How's her job going?" I asked.

"She's on medical leave right now. Her knee ballooned from fluid retention, and she can't walk on it or bend it without terrible pain." He made a rude noise in disgust. "Have you ever heard of a husband *and* a wife both being on medical leave at the same time? Shee-it."

"Jesus, Todd, I haven't." What a mess. I felt sorry for their toddler daughter, who had to feel the stress. Annie's high-pitched wails and mucous-choked gasps were quieting down at last.

"I swear I'm going crazy," T-bone ranted, "with Mary being home all the time. We can't have a normal conversation, she's so fucking nuts. Sure, she's under a lot of pressure right now, but, hey, that's reality! As soon as all this is straightened out, our worries will be over."

I watched Todd as he continued his tirade about the insurance company and the hotel, plus tyrants and oppressors not connected to his claim, as far as I could tell. Most of it didn't make sense because he was so high on coke and whatever else he had in his system.

I tried to stir up compassion for him, but all I could find in my heart was revulsion because he had crossed too many lines. With his bad decisions and excessive drug and alcohol use, T-bone had transformed himself into a half-psychotic monster with a brain so primitive in its drive for pleasure, he was hardly recognizable as human.

Todd was, in 3-D and Technicolor, the embodiment of what could and did go wrong in Las Vegas. To me, he epitomized how the city, polluted by lust and greed and temptation, could destroy visitors and residents alike.

T-bone had used every temptation available in Las Vegas to annihilate himself with a vengeance.

Had he been on a USMC special assignment to assassinate the enemy, he could not have done a more thorough or efficient job. All that remained of the vitamin-popping, water-swigging, hyperactive health nut who had been my partner were pale ruins spread across the sofa pillows. And he was too potent and poisonous for me to stay with him in the same room for more than a few minutes.

I jumped up from my chair.

"You all right, man?" he asked. "You look sort of weird."

"I'm okay. Probably just nerves. I've made huge changes in my life a couple times before, but I was really pumped up about them. This time I'm filled with fear, I don't—"

"Hey, what time is it?"

I looked at my watch and told him.

"Cool. Where's the remote?"

I searched around and found it within a heap of newspapers, back issues of *Sports Illustrated,* and a half-empty bottle of vodka.

"And pass me the OxyContin® and the vodka." He pointed at the coffee table.

He took his dose, washed it down, and then aimed the remote at the television. He repositioned himself slowly, painfully, and settled in. Time for me to escape.

"Well, partner—"

The doorbell rang, and he and I looked at each other.

"I can't answer," Mary called down the stairs. "Annie's in the tub."

"Get it for me, man," T-bone asked.

I walked to the front door. On the step were two clean-cut men around my age, wearing suits and ties. I figured they were canvassing the neighborhood to hand out religious pamphlets. Then one asked if I were Todd.

"Uh, no. He's inside," I said.

"Who is it, man?" T-bone called from the sofa as the men pushed past me, badges shining from their small black-leather wallet.

Remembering everyone's advice about not getting involved, I hung back but listened as the lawmen introduced themselves and handed Todd a subpoena requiring him to defend himself in court. The state of Nevada had charged him with fraud.

"You gotta be shittin' me, man!" I heard him shout.

Mary limped down the stairs, gripping the railing to support her weight as the agents crossed the foyer toward the front door. Her eyes were wide with fear. "Who are they, Jay?" she asked me.

"Can't you see I'm in pain?" T-bone yelled, but the men kept walking.

Behind Mary, Annie stood at the top of the stairs, her compact little body wrapped in a white towel. Her hair hung in wet strings, and her little hands were balled into fists as she wailed. Mary looked down toward the living room, where her husband was screaming, then up at her sobbing daughter. She did not know which way to go. Her dark eyes pleaded with me: Jay. Please. Take care of Todd.

My heart broke for Mary. Of course I would help her. She couldn't abandon Annie, and T-bone needed someone to calm his ass down. Anyway, helping people had been my lifelong inclination. I took a step toward the living room door.

Suddenly I stopped. I knew I had to get out of there. I'd had enough of trying to save T-bone from himself. If I stayed for even five minutes, I'd be listening to his rage until he passed out. Then Mary would sob on my shoulder for the rest of the night.

I had to save myself, now, or I might end up throwing T-bone's pills down my own throat.

I walked outside, took a deep breath, got in my car, and pulled away from the curb without so much as a glance at their house.

I drove to the Strip. I wanted to take a last look at what had been my life. Only when I had all the resorts and casinos in my rearview mirror would I finally be able to put all the crap behind me . . . everything except myself.

My car went over a bump, and the small metal box on the floor of the passenger side bounced, attracting my attention. The ten grand locked inside had taken me years to save. I had lost everything else.

I felt overwhelmed and morose. Doubting my ability to drive safely, I turned sharply into the parking lot of the next casino on my side of the road. I pulled the Lincoln into a space and shut off the ignition, then locked the doors. A flashing neon sign overhead flooded the car with orange, then left it in darkness as I reached for the cashbox and set it on my lap.

I tried to gather my thoughts. The visit with T-bone had rattled me, and only now was my pulse slowing toward normal. Maybe heading for the Strip after T-bone's house hadn't been the most brilliant idea. I shook my head, thinking of my partner. We would be friends again someday. He and I had shared so much, we would always be connected—of that much I was certain.

I also knew that Vegas had the power to destroy. I'd sensed its current running through me while I was at work; I'd felt its vibration under the sidewalk wherever I went. I had seen what it had done to any number of people. I stared down at the box in my lap. How could I be sure the money hadn't absorbed that destructive charge? If it had, then the stash was capable of poisoning my every endeavor. I'd be goddamned if I'd let that happen.

I lay my hands on the lid, but its cool smoothness revealed nothing. What the fuck, I decided. I've lost everything else, so why not lose this, too?

I grabbed the box and went inside.

I felt strangely at peace as I walked toward the blackjack tables. The room may have been filled with excitement and possibility, but I felt none of it. A thousand players may have been laughing, but I heard nothing. In the past this would have been the place I could stop thinking about whatever was bringing me down. Tonight, there would be no forgetting.

Dealers came in two varieties—either sociable blondes with long acrylic fingernails or plain, bored-looking Asian women. I was in the mood for the latter.

I sat at the first table with a quiet dealer. I opened my box. "I'll bet ten thousand," I said.

She looked up quickly. "Change for ten thousand," she called out, which brought a pit boss on the run.

I knew what to expect—these bosses were highly trained in customer service. He wanted to be my next best friend.

He smiled warmly. "You want them in thousands?" he asked, referring to the chips.

I nodded.

"Are you a guest here?" he asked. "I can take care of your room—"

"No."

"Can I comp you dinner, then?" He counted out the chips.

"No, thanks."

"A host?"

I placed all ten chips into the small betting circle.

The boss stayed at the dealer's shoulder, and I could almost feel the eye in the sky staring down at us from the ceiling.

I was intent upon losing the money. "If I win this hand," I told the dealer, "I'm going to let it ride one time."

She looked up, and for a split second our eyes met. Her nod was almost imperceptible.

I waited for the cards.

The pit boss gave me a quick glance and a smile. He was staging himself, prepared to treat me like a king so I would keep coming back to this hotel—the more I played, the more I would lose. He wanted his casino to be my home away from home, but I had no home.

The dealer threw the cards: a seven for me and a ten for her. She dealt two more cards facedown for each of us. I lifted my card. It was a ten. I had seventeen.

The odds were against me since the dealer was already showing a ten. I had to stay put.

She lifted her facedown card. It was a two. She had to take at least one more card.

I held my breath as she dealt herself a ten. I won ten thousand dollars in seconds.

My hands were frozen. I felt a rush of emotion. I wanted to cry and rage at the same time. This money was the lure, the temptation, the hope.

I looked at the money, then up at the dealer. "Let it ride," I confirmed.

Her gaze flicked toward my friend the pit boss. He nodded to her, then looked at me. "Good luck, pal," he said.

Fuck you, I thought as I smiled back.

The dealer started the next hand, one card for each of us. The king of diamonds for me, and the ten of spades for her. She dealt the next two cards facedown.

I lifted my down card. The queen of hearts. As I stared at my card, the queen seemed to smile back at me.

The dealer turned her card over. A five. She had to draw another card. Her movements were in slow motion as she turned the next card. Two of spades.

I took a deep breath—my first deep breath in what seemed like hours or maybe years. I turned my card over. The dealer's eyes widened, and she pushed the chips at me. Forty thousand dollars.

It was time for me to go.

I drove all night. The California highway ended at the ocean. I parked the Lincoln and grabbed the black box on the passenger seat and walked down to the beach. The sun was rising as I opened the box to look at my winnings—thirty thousand, plus my original ten.

As the sky lightened I sat on the cool sand, breathed in the salt air, and stared at the money. A few hours before, I had believed the money was cursed. It represented everything I had endured in my love-hate relationship with Las Vegas. If I had lost it, I would have been relieved.

Now I felt different about what lay in front of me. Suddenly I had hope.

In Memory of

T-bone and Sam.

Jay Rankin didn't research Las Vegas, he lived it. His six years as an MGM Grand doorman gave the insider's view of real Las Vegas life, the grit behind the glitz. Jay reveals a Vegas few people know exists.

Jay hosted a weekly television show, "Las Vegas Business Week." That media experience and his connections won him the ambassador's job out of 1700 applicants.

Jay holds an advanced degree in Psychology. He began writing in 1993 and is currently working on his second book about his life after escaping Vegas. He resides in Los Angeles, California.

Contact: Jay@JaysLasVegas.com
www.JaysLasVegas.com